"The Object Lessons series achieves something very close to magic: the books take ordinary—even banal—objects and animate them with a rich history of invention, political struggle, science, and popular mythology. Filled with fascinating details and conveyed in sharp, accessible prose, the books make the everyday world come to life. Be warned: once you've read a few of these, you'll start walking around your house, picking up random objects, and musing aloud: 'I wonder what the story is behind this thing?'"

Steven Johnson, author of *Where Good Ideas Come From* and *How We Got to Now*

"In 1957 the French critic and semiotician Roland Barthes published *Mythologies*, a groundbreaking series of essays in which he analysed the popular culture of his day, from laundry detergent to the face of Greta Garbo, professional wrestling to the Citroën DS. This series of short books, Object Lessons, continues the tradition."

Melissa Harrison, *Financial Times*

"Though short, at roughly 25,000 words apiece, these books are anything but slight."

Marina Benjamin, *New Statesman*

The joy of the series, of reading *Remote Control*, *Golf Ball*, *Driver's License*, *Drone*, *Silence*, *Glass*, *Refrigerator*, *Hotel*, and *Waste* (more titles are listed as forthcoming) in quick succession, lies in encountering the various turns through which each of their authors has been put by his or her object. As for Benjamin, so for the authors of the series, the object predominates, sits squarely center stage, directs the action. The object decides the genre, the chronology, and the limits of the study. Accordingly, the author has to take her cue from the *thing* she chose or that chose her. The result is a wonderfully uneven series of books, each one a *thing* unto itself."

Julian Yates, *Los Angeles Review of Books*

The Object Lessons project, edited by game theory legend Ian Bogost and cultural studies academic Christopher Schaberg, commissions short essays and small, beautiful books about everyday objects from shipping containers to toast. *The Atlantic* hosts a collection of "mini object-lessons"… More substantive is Bloomsbury's collection of small, gorgeously designed books that delve into their subjects in much more depth."

Cory Doctorow, *Boing Boing*

OBJECT LESSONS

A book series about the hidden lives of ordinary things.

Series Editors:

Ian Bogost and Christopher Schaberg

Advisory Board:

Sara Ahmed, Jane Bennett, Jeffrey Jerome Cohen, Johanna Drucker, Raiford Guins, Graham Harman, renée hoogland, Pam Houston, Eileen Joy, Douglas Kahn, Daniel Miller, Esther Milne, Timothy Morton, Kathleen Stewart, Nigel Thrift, Rob Walker, Michele White.

In association with

Georgia Tech | Center for Media Studies

BOOKS IN THE SERIES

bread

SCOTT CUTLER SHERSHOW

Bloomsbury Academic
An imprint of Bloomsbury Publishing Inc

B L O O M S B U R Y
NEW YORK · LONDON · OXFORD · NEW DELHI · SYDNEY

Bloomsbury Academic

An imprint of Bloomsbury Publishing Inc

<table>
<tr><td>1385 Broadway</td><td>50 Bedford Square</td></tr>
<tr><td>New York</td><td>London</td></tr>
<tr><td>NY 10018</td><td>WC1B 3DP</td></tr>
<tr><td>USA</td><td>UK</td></tr>
</table>

www.bloomsbury.com

**BLOOMSBURY and the Diana logo are trademarks of
Bloomsbury Publishing Plc**

First published 2016

Library of Congress Cataloging-in-Publication Data
Names: Shershow, Scott Cutler, 1953– author.
Title: Bread / Scott Cutler Shershow.
Description: New York: Bloomsbury Academic, 2016. | Series: Object lessons |
Includes bibliographical references and index.
Identifiers: LCCN 2015043362 (print) | LCCN 2016000360 (ebook) |
ISBN 9781501307447 (paperback) | ISBN 9781501307454 (ePub) |
ISBN 9781501307461 (ePDF)
Subjects: LCSH: Bread–Popular works. | BISAC: SOCIAL SCIENCE /
Anthropology / Cultural. | SOCIAL SCIENCE / Media Studies. | PHILOSOPHY /
Aesthetics. Classification: LCC TX558.B7 S53 2016 (print) | LCC TX558.B7
(ebook) | DDC 641.81/5–dc23
LC record available at http://lccn.loc.gov/2015043362

ISBN: PB: 978-1-5013-0744-7
ePub: 978-1-5013-0745-4
ePDF: 978-1-5013-0746-1

Series: Object Lessons

Cover design: Alice Marwick
Cover image © Alice Marwick

Typeset by Deanta Global Publishing Services, Chennai, India
Printed and bound in the United States of America

CONTENTS

1 BREAD BOOK

Believing the strangest things,
Loving the alien.

—DAVID BOWIE[1]

When some traditional breads, especially crusty breads such as the famous French *baguette*, first come out of the oven, they make a subtle crackling sound for a few moments. Each loaf's spongy interior contracts as it cools, pulling on the stiff crust that encloses it and making it crack, causing a soft, sibilant whispering or sighing that, even when many loaves come out of the oven all at once, one must always strain a little to hear. This sound is beloved by bakers, who refer to it as the loaves "singing."[2]

But if the loaves sing, what are they singing about? If they speak, what do they say? That is one way to describe the question to be asked, in a variety of ways, in this book.

I am drawn to such a question and such a book by what I can only describe as a strange and unexpected passion. A moment came—I cannot quite say how or why—when I realized I was in love with bread. No doubt that sounds like a strange thing to say. For one thing, I had of course eaten bread all of my life, like most people in most parts of the world; and had even baked bread, sporadically and unsystematically, since my teens. I still have my stained and dog-eared copy of James Beard's famous *Beard on Bread* (1973), a book commonly claimed to have introduced a whole generation of Americans to home baking. Next to it today are many other more recent books by the superb bakers who emerged in the artisanal "bread revolution" of the 1990s and beyond, whose recipes, in my continuing passion for baking, I have poured over, compared, and followed in the kitchen, sometimes even successfully.[3]

In other words, I had always, in a simple sense, liked bread, as something to make and to eat; and been interested in bread as an object with complex meanings and a complicated history. But just as it is often difficult in personal relationships to know exactly when love begins, so I cannot pinpoint the moment when I knew I was in love with bread. I am not even sure whether I am writing this book because I fell love with bread, or whether I fell in love with bread when I began to write this book. Does it make any difference?

In any case, what captivates me most is not so much bread as a product, nor even an idea, but as a process and an experience. And the passion I explore in these pages is not (or at least not merely) what you may be expecting: the easy and comfortable pleasures of hearth and home, the warm oven on a cold day, the irresistible savor of a freshly baked loaf. Such images are in every sense *familiar* and *common*: the very figures of family, community, and well-being.

But what I want to share with you here is a darker, stranger and more dangerous love: a love of the *alien*.

Why would I describe the homely and familiar experience of bread in this way? To begin with, at the time of this writing, bread remains slightly alien to me simply because I'm still learning all the myriad mysteries and nuances of the bread-baking process. One might say that bread is both quite easy and quite difficult to make. On the one hand, simple breads can be made by anyone in an average home kitchen, and with only a modest investment of time and effort will equal or surpass, in nutritional value and eating pleasure, anything you can buy wrapped in plastic at the grocery store. On the other hand, the finest artisanal breads are the product of an extraordinary and intricate craft that one learns only gradually, and perhaps never masters absolutely. For an amateur like myself, to watch a professional baker at work is as humbling as it is enthralling. Yet even the very finest of bakers will sometimes acknowledge that the process of baking is not exactly, or not simply, one of *mastery*: for one does not so much *make* bread as work *with* it.

In a great many other ways as well, bread—which "appears at first sight to be an extremely obvious, trivial thing"—can be shown to be "a very strange thing, abounding in metaphysical subtleties and theological niceties."[4] The reader who has noticed I make this point by repurposing the famous opening lines of Karl Marx's chapter in *Capital* on "The Fetishism of the Commodity and its Secret" may take this as a precaution. For of course it is finally because bread does present itself, quite literally, as the *master* of so many—the "staff of life," the ultimate staple commodity, an object marking the very line of survival itself—that bread as either an object or an idea has accumulated such overwhelming symbolic power. This is obviously why the word and image "bread" often signifies *value* itself, and refers metaphorically either to food in general, or to something like "livelihood," in expressions such as "breadwinner," "taking the bread out of his mouth," and so forth. Similarly, both "bread" and "dough" have been used as slang words for money. And no wonder, because it is precisely in societies like ours, societies radically divided along lines of wealth and poverty, that bread becomes (as Piero Camporesi writes), "a polyvalent object on which life, death and dreams depend . . . the culminating point and instrument, real and symbolic, of existence itself."[5] To think about bread at all is therefore necessarily also to dream of what the utopian socialist Peter Kropotkin calls, in the title of his most famous text, *The Conquest of Bread*: the unappeasable demand for a world in which

> there is not single man who lacks bread, not a single woman compelled to stand with the wearied crowd outside the bakehouse-door, that haply a coarse loaf may be thrown to her in charity, not a single child pining for want of food.[6]

And so, however much I love bread, however much I have struggled to master the making of it, and relished the flavors and fragrances of each of its disparate moments of existence (the grain, the dough, the loaf, the slice), I cannot ignore the more difficult side of its histories and meanings. Even for those of us who have never known real privation, our individual and collective experience of bread can never be entirely separated from violence and scarcity, from famine and dearth.

Yet if bread thus necessarily serves as the very symbol, figure, or instance of the "iron law" of economy (what Marx calls the realm of Necessity), by the same token it also figures the realm of Freedom. The medieval peasants in France known as the *Jacquerie* revolted against their masters with the slogan *le pain se lève*—the bread rises. As Kropotkin writes, all "utopian dreamers," first and last, "shall have to consider the question of daily bread."[7]

I also have other senses in mind when I speak of my love of bread as a love of the alien. For example, Ian Bogost (one of the co-editors of this book series) proposes that the word *alien* be used philosophically to refer to *all* objects as a way of denoting their inaccessibility to human beings, how they finally escape our knowledge and perception. Bogost cites another contemporary philosopher, Nicholas Rescher, who speculates that the extraterrestrial beings long dreamed of both in science and science fiction might be so radically different from us as to be absolutely incomprehensible. Taking this idea even farther, Bogost suggests that the figure of the "alien" should not apply merely to the literal extraterrestrial or "space-alien"—nor even, as one might venture to add, to the noncitizen, the migrant or "illegal alien." For Bogost, "The true alien . . . is not hidden in the darkness of the outer cosmos . . . but in plain sight, everywhere, in everything."[8] Timothy Morton, similarly, has proposed that the phrase the "strange stranger," which he had used originally to refer to the "uncanny, radically unpredictable quality" of nonhuman life, should also be applied to *all* objects. This strangeness of objects, Morton suggests (in an argument drawn in part from the related work of Graham Harman) finally stems from the way in which they *withdraw* from us, from one another, and indeed, from all relations.[9] By thinking this way, and by thus attending to the radical strangeness and alterity of all objects, Bogost, Morton, Harman, and other like-minded contemporary thinkers claim that philosophy can finally overcome, once and for all, the anthropomorphism or "human-centric" perspective, that, it is further argued, has fatally limited it since its beginnings.

The observations I make here have been shaped in part by Bogost's vision of the incommunicability of all things, and Morton's sense of the strangeness with which objects confront us. But I also draw on the thought known as deconstruction and the work of Jacques Derrida, for whom (to summarize far too briefly) anthropocentrism is not the kind of problem that can be overcome simply by declaring one has done so. As Derrida warns, in an essay from almost half a century ago, "the step 'outside philosophy' is much more difficult to conceive, than is generally imagined by those who think they made it long ago with cavalier ease."[10] I would thus join Derrida in suggesting that the vexed frontiers between the so-called human and the so-called animal, or even between the animate and the inanimate, the subjective and the objective—although they ought always to be troubled, questioned, redrawn, and rethought, and although this work remains an urgent and interminable responsibility—cannot simply be lifted or erased in one cataclysmic gesture, once and for all. The task of thought, Derrida suggests in various texts, is to *solicit* such trouble and such questioning (playing on the word's Latin root, *solicitare*, to tremble). But this is quite another thing than to simply reduce the difference between, let's say, a human being and a loaf of bread.

(Or perhaps, much more simply and personally, I just cannot force myself to think in terms of "withdrawal" with regard to objects such as flour, yeast, dough, and bread— things that literally coexist with me, things that have filled my hands, my mouth, my time and my space, things that metabolize *for* me even as I later metabolize them, things I have *digested* in every possible sense of the word. The comedian Maria Bamford once described a fantasy of being "dipped into a vat of warm, rising bread dough": an experience, she implies, that might be as pleasurable as sex.[11] Would you join me, dear reader, in imagining an *erotics* of bread?[12] And if so then let me ask: Would this be *escaping* anthropocentrism . . . or *succumbing* to it?)

In any case, however, when I speak of my love of bread as a love of the alien, I also mean something more like what Frances E. Dolan calls the "dangerous familiar": that is, an absolute and sometimes violent Otherness that sometimes presents itself at the very center of the home, the hearth, and the heart.[13] This time, I have in mind a simple fact about the making of many kinds of bread whose radical strangeness cannot quite be extinguished even by our scientific and practical familiarity with all of its mechanisms and details. The most familiar kind of bread—the kind made of nothing more than flour, water, salt, and yeast, which are mixed, fermented, shaped and baked—is the product of a remarkable cooperation or symbiosis between human beings and a variety of microorganisms. This so-called "leavened" bread has been given its shape and appealing lightness by a combination of certain peculiar properties of the starch and protein molecules in the wheat, and by the microbial action of yeast (a fungus) and lacto-bacteria, who themselves cooperate symbiotically in the process known as "fermentation."

Making bread thus quite literally involves a deliberate manipulation of organic processes otherwise associated with decay and decomposition. Accordingly, across a long tradition of discourse and social practice, fermentation has been seen almost as often as a vaguely frightening form of contamination as it has a benevolent miracle. Perhaps this is no wonder, since, as we all know, some versions of these same microorganisms (or their cousins) can also make human beings very sick or even kill them. The development of an industrial model of mass-produced bread in the twentieth century (something commonly deplored by practically everyone who writes about bread today) was, at least in part, designed specifically to shield from the senses of the consumer all traces of the messy biological details of bread making. Nevertheless, either as a concrete object or as an image, symbol, or metaphor, as we shall see, this so-called "staff of life" proves to be haunted by a certain figure of *death*.

In our times, another current of thought has emerged that regards bread as a fundamental human *mistake*. This is argued in a variety of ways leading to more than one conclusion. On one side, adherents of a so-called "stone-age" or "paleo" diet, which has become popular in the last decade or so in the United States and elsewhere in the developed world, emulate the diet of "hunter-gatherers" from the Paleolithic period, especially by rejecting with the fervor and passion of a religion any and all products of grain agriculture. An even larger group of people, estimated to be as many as one third of Americans, avoid bread because they have been convinced that of one of its distinctive ingredients, the protein gluten, is bad for them—notwithstanding a scientific consensus that there is nothing whatsoever wrong with gluten for the vast majority of human beings. Today a veritable industry of cookbooks and "gluten-free" products has developed to confirm the new nutritional creed and fulfill its self-formulated requirements. On the other side, other writers, motivated this time as much by political and economic concerns as nutritional ones, have gone so far as to argue that agriculture itself was a profound wrong turn for humanity, for, in making possible the maintenance of settled human communities, it also eventually enabled state power, poverty, social distinction, and all the rest of the ills that attend the modern world.

A love of the alien indeed! When I started this book, I expected that one challenge might be to avoid the trap of easy sentimentality, those images of hearth and home I mentioned a moment ago. It turns out, on the contrary, that at least in some people's eyes, I am in love with a monster, an indigestible poison, the number one culprit for cancer and capitalism, obesity and war, and pretty much everything else that has ever gone wrong in the whole human adventure. Although I am obviously skeptical about the claims of these "paleo" and "gluten-free" dieters, I (who am no scientist but a literary scholar and amateur philosopher) will offer no definitive refutation of their claims. At most, I will suggest that this new rejection of bread partakes of a familiar cultural nostalgia about the irretrievable past. Perhaps it even echoes the ancient association of yeast and corruption and expresses an unconscious distaste for this dangerous familiar: the literally alien beings who live, work, and die with us in our homes, our bakeries, and our bodies.

And so the strangest thing about bread is not some objective *quality* immanent in the dough I knead, in the loaf I slice, or in the slice I butter and eat, nor even some subjective experience of these various objects and actions. It is, rather, that the thought of bread is so often, and in so many ways, a thought of the Self and the Other. As I have just suggested, the simple act of eating or making bread finally links us to all those who have been or are deprived of it. At another level, bread also involves an intimate interaction between human beings and various examples of what we might call, following Donna Haraway, "companion species."[14] Since Haraway's primary instance of a companion species is the dog, the term may perhaps seem incongruous to apply to yeast cells and bacteria. Yet, as Haraway and many others have observed, the very word "companion" derives from the Latin *cum panis*, "with bread." This Latin phrase and its modern English derivate seem to indicate a small shift of meaning from the object at issue to the human subjects who will consume it. The *being-with* designated is not so much a relation of human beings to bread, but the sharing of it by "companions" who will, in the conventional phrase, "break bread" together. Just as bread has often been a collective thing in its practical conditions (the grain ground by the neighborhood miller, the bread baked in communal ovens, the loaves themselves usually large enough to invite or require sharing), so bread in its very idea commonly serves as the very token, rubric, or occasion for the "with" of companionship itself.

Even in itself bread is also the ultimate transformational food, something always in process of changing from one thing to another. As the great contemporary baker and baking teacher Peter Reinhart writes, among the myriad varieties of bread in the world, the one universal thing is "transformation"—a process by which "a tasteless pile of flour, like sawdust on the tongue, is miraculously transformed into a multilayered series of flavors and textures."[15]

Accordingly, when I claim to write of this object, bread, what exactly am I referring to? Some of the myriad kinds of bread in the world are so completely different from one another in taste and appearance as to seem to be entirely different things. The category "bread" encompasses a spectrum that might include things as disparate as unleavened flatbreads (ranging from the Indian *roti*, *chapati*, and *paratha*, to the Middle Eastern *pita* and *lavash*, to the corn or flour *tortillas* of the Americas, to *matzah*, unleavened bread baked for the Jewish ritual of *Pesach*), "quick" breads leavened with reactive chemicals instead of yeast (such as American cornbread or Irish soda bread), Navajo fry bread, buckwheat pancakes, bagels, hot cross buns, croissants, crackers, pizza . . . and so on, a seemingly inexhaustible variety. Even in Asia or Latin America, whose societies were respectively grounded in the agriculture of rice or corn (maize), traditional wheat breads of various kinds are not uncommon, and European-style breads are widely manufactured and consumed today.

So where exactly does one draw the line around the category "bread"? It is commonly assumed that early human beings consumed grain either in the form of porridges or "pottages," or as simple flatbreads, in which the same mush or "batter" of grain would be formed into cakes to be cooked on a hot stone. Because such a mush tends to ferment naturally if left for any time at all, some of these primitive flatbreads were probably at least slightly leavened (like the sourdough pancakes in contemporary Ethiopian cuisine). Even the simplest flatbread or pancake seems to the eye and taste to be a quite different thing than a bowl of porridge; and even though the two might have been made with identical ingredients, they will (especially if the bread is leavened) prove to be different in their chemical and biological substance due to the action of the fermentation and the "browning" on the surface of the baked or griddled cake or loaf.

But notwithstanding all this, and even if there were only a single kind of bread in the world, should the object "bread" be understood as the loaf, the slice, or even the crumb? (On the cover of this book, for example, all three of these are pictured.) Although all objects exist only in time (which is obvious), bread presents itself to us with particular vividness as something always in process of turning into something else. Where does one draw the line between the porridge and the cake, between the mush and the flatbread, between the dough and the loaf? Such a line is no more than an indeterminable instant within a dynamic and essentially endless process of transformation.

It is thus in the vexed conceptual space where "words" and "things" somehow cohabit, the domain of thought, language, discourse, and especially *metaphor* (the all-important mechanism of linguistic substitution by which a words, things, and ideas change places with one another), that my titular object seems to explode in a vertiginous spiral of multiple meanings. And so we are going to have to think about *manna* from heaven and "daily bread," about the communion wafer and the bread of affliction, about breads of life and breads of death—although we will be able to approach some of these meanings only indirectly or from more than one direction. As a metaphor, bread has more meanings than one can count, meanings that both multiply and fade over its long history. Especially in the realms of ritual and religion, the myriad figural and metaphoric meanings of bread proliferate so readily and in so many directions as to make it a kind of master signifier, a figure *of* figurality. Doesn't bread seem to be the very thing that always gestures toward the impossible fracture of idea and act, sign and referent, metaphor and thing? For example: we have long told ourselves that we do not live by bread *alone*; but this famous saying would not signify at all if not for our certain knowledge that we must have bread (or something like it) to *live*.

In all this, to use a word with the valence given to it in the thought of Derrida, bread's myriad meanings *disseminate* in unpredictable ways.[16] I bring this up because, on the one hand, the experience of trying to make bread has helped me understand some of Derrida's arguments in a newly vivid way—to understand them (as Shakespeare puts it) *feelingly.* And, on the other hand, Derrida's arguments, in turn, have helped bring into focus some of what I find so special and strange about the process and experience of bread. We need not, of course, rehearse all the details of Derrida's argument involving this term *dissemination* (one of a series of such terms in Derrida's work), and can take it as referring, in brief, to the process by which everything distributes and transforms itself by inscribing itself in time and space. Only a little more broadly, *dissemination* gestures toward a principle of non-self-identity that affects everything that exists in time. Since each moment can only appear by disappearing, there is no moment, "now," in which any "object"—*including* so-called "subjects" like us—is entirely self-present, *in* the present.

The process and experience of making bread seems to me to be a vivid and intimate model or instance of *dissemination* in this philosophic sense. In baking, the smallest of differences in space (the shaping and rising of the dough), or time (the duration of each stage in its making) have enormous consequences for the look, taste, and general quality of the finished bread. One fermentation or two, long or short rises, smaller or larger lumps of dough, warmer or colder ambient temperatures . . . all of these affect the finished product in big ways. The same recipe can come out differently depending on where you are on the terrestrial globe, what time of day or season of the year it is, how strong and skillful your hands are, and so forth. Correspondingly, as the baker's joke goes, the most important and most expensive ingredient of all in the whole process of bread making is always *time*.[17] Most so-called artisanal approaches to baking recommend allowing the dough to undergo long, slow fermentations, which produces a range of complex flavors in the finished loaf. Even in industrial bread making, the temporal dimension remains central—even though it is regarded as a *problem* to be overcome, rather than a condition of possibility. How fast *can* one speedup the rising of the dough, and thus the time from dough to loaf? And then, on the other side of the process, how long can one manage to extend the "shelf life" of the finished product?

I observe, finally, that the word *dissemination* is itself a metaphor drawn from agriculture and thus intimately related to the history and experience of bread. "To disseminate" originally meant to scatter seeds: for example, the lexicographer Thomas Blount defines it in 1656 as "to sow here and there, to spread abroad."[18] This word can also be also used in a technical sense to describe how spores (such as those of yeast) will, given the right conditions, diffuse themselves in an appropriate medium (such as a paste of grain and water). Thus bread—both as object and as idea, and, so to speak, both in its *making* and in its *breaking*—is always the product of an intricate dance of time and space whose being quite literally *disseminates*. I think this may be, above all, why I love it, and why—as I hope to show you with this necessarily scattershot set of reflections—bread always seems to be an object at once so familiar and so alien, so common yet so strange.

2 BREAD DANCE

When I first got serious about bread I attended a weeklong class in professional baking; and when I came home I had with me more than a dozen loaves that I had baked in the last day or so, far more than I could eat or even freeze. Some friends with twin toddlers were nice enough to take some of the bread off my hands. Later that evening they sent me a brief video of the twins, each holding a piece of bread as they danced and cavorted wildly. A voice is heard saying: "What are you doing?" and the children reply, almost in unison, "We're doing the bread-dance, the bread-dance!"

The phrase made my mind pirouette in many directions at once. It was pretty much impossible not to imagine, at least for a moment, that some ancient harvest festival or ritual of thanksgiving for the gift of bread had re-presented itself in person via some inexplicable mechanism of collective memory. Was I witnessing some mysteriously reborn version of the Eleusinian Mysteries—the great celebration of the Bread in ancient Greece, in which the first fruits of the harvested grain would be offered back to their source, the goddess Demeter? Many remnants of these ritual practices persist in the modern world, from the Shawnee Indian "bread dance" still celebrated each year in spring and fall, or the Macedonian "bread dance" in which a newly married couple breaks in two a large round loaf of sweet yeast bread called a *koluk*; not to mention the "barn dances" or "grange dances" in the United Kingdom or United States whose distant origins in harvest festival still haunt these names just as the bread-goddess Ceres still haunts the word "cereal."[1]

But the joy of this particular bread dance also rhymed with what I have to admit was my own emotion about all these variously shaped loaves I had made. Ironically, I knew enough about baking that I could not ignore their imperfections: this one a bit misshapen, that one slightly overbaked, and so forth. Yet even such recognition at most tempered an overpowering feeling whose source remained obscure and that I could not quite name or describe. To call it joy or pride would not be wrong, but seems insufficient; and this strange emotion somehow shouldered its way past any other feeling. I felt light on my feet, as though I too was ready to dance.

Michael Pollan, who in a series of justly celebrated books has established himself as perhaps our premier contemporary writer about food, describes the similar sense of achievement he felt on baking his first loaf of bread. He acknowledges that he "spent some time trying to parse the almost absurd pride I felt about this loaf and various others I've baked since." And, as he asks, "What is it about a loaf of bread" that should strike us as such a signal achievement, one that goes beyond the simple pride of cooking (and therefore having) something good to eat?[2]

In trying to answer his own question, Pollan suggests, first, that he is feeling an "aesthetic" satisfaction because, unlike many forms of food, a loaf of bread is obviously an artifact, something radically transformed by his labor. As he writes,

> A loaf of bread is something new added to the world, an edged object wrested from the flux of nature—and specifically from the living, shifting, Dionysian swamp that is dough. Bread is the Apollonian food.

Second, baking bread gave him a "sense of personal competence." Despite the importance of bread in our diet, for the vast majority of us "the ability to make this necessary thing has passed out of our hands and into those of specialists." The simple fact that baking bread

> is now solidly within the orbit of my competence, that my hands now know how to transform a pile of cheap flour and free water (free microbes, too!) into something that will not only nourish but also give so much pleasure to my family, changes everything. Or at least changes me. I am a little less dependent, and a little more self-reliant, than I used to be.[3]

These observations came back to my mind when I was con-fronted by the strangely familiar image of a *dance of bread*.

Let us ponder Pollan's question—what is the source of the powerful emotions raised by baking bread?—a little longer, as he invites us to do by marking it as a tricky one.

Our contemporary understanding of the classical terms cited in Pollan's first passage above comes largely from Nietzsche's *The Birth of Tragedy*, a book arguing that the greatness of classical Greek tragedy, as of all art, stems from a process by which a Dionysian ecstasy (often associated with music and dance) is transfigured by an Apollonian harmony and order (often associated with architecture). Anyone who has ever worked with bread will probably understand how this schema might seem to apply to the experience: how the formless ooze of the dough is transformed into the coherent solidity of the loaf. The extraordinary *rising* of bread, its radical transmutation from formlessness to form, can be deemed Apollonian all the more in that "bread" often serves as a rubric or symbol of something like civilization or culture, of humanity's struggle (as Marx puts it) to wrest a realm of Freedom from a realm of Necessity. The Old English word for bread is *hláf*, the source of the modern English word "loaf." Some scholars derive *hláf* from *hlífian*, a word that could either be a verb meaning "to rise high" or a noun meaning "tower."[4] H. E. Jacob, in his idiosyncratic but remarkable *Six Thousand Years of Bread: Its Holy and Unholy History*, first published in 1944 and still in print today, speculates, by contrast, that *hláf* derives, via consonantal shift, from *gleba* or *glebe*, meaning soil, earth, clod, or lump. Thus, Jacob suggests, "The end product, the *bread loaf*, is faithful to its origin in the *gleba*, the cultivated soil."[5] In these twin etymologies, bread seems again to be a quintessential figure or symbol of the human encounter with nature, something that essentially *rises*—both *from* the earth and *in* the loaf. (One might even speculate that the use of the verb "to rise" as a metaphor for evolution and development—as in a phrase such as "the rise of the Roman Empire"—is conditioned by the familiar image of rising bread.) Bread thus presents itself, as Pollan writes elsewhere, as an object essentially *raised* from "the earthbound subsistence of gruel to something so fundamentally transformed as to hint at human and even divine transcendence."[6]

It is a compelling vision, and I feel almost ungenerous to question it, however slightly. And yet, in envisioning bread as a sort of Apollonian monument rising out of the Dionysian swamp of the dough, do we perhaps risk reducing Nietzsche's opposition to simply one between "nature" and "culture," or even "matter" and "form?" Moreover, since Nietzsche's schema is intended to apply to the work of art, we might first have to ask whether it can be applied to a foodstuff at all, even one such as bread that is sometimes the product of considerable artistry and skill. In Kant's aesthetic theory, for example, a loaf of bread, no matter how well made, could only be an instance of "the agreeable," something to be fundamentally contrasted to "the beautiful." All merely agreeable things, for Kant, involve the fulfillment of some personal interest (such as satisfying one's hunger); only the judgment of beauty is "disinterested."[7]

But my point at the moment is merely that Dionysius is just as much a product of human civilization as Apollo; and that dough is just as much "culture" as bread. At a climactic moment of Sophocles' *Antigone,* the chorus invokes together the god "of many names," Dionysius, and the "ruler of Eleusis whose valleys embosom all mankind"—that is, Demeter, the bread goddess.[8] The fragmentary accounts of the mysteries of Eleusis suggest that Dionysius was also invoked as a central figure in the ritual.[9] Correspondingly, the joy of bread partakes as much of intoxication as achievement, and the *experience* of bread as a whole, if one can even speak of such a thing, is not so much an Apollonian monument as a Dionysian dance of time and space taking us to the very limits of our being and beyond.

In fact, although this is obviously a different point, rising dough is quite literally what we call a *culture*: a living colony of microorganisms. That the term should be the same as the one I have just used to refer to the domain of human practice, all that opposes a so-called "nature," is not a coincidence. For the last two centuries or so, via a many-sided intellectual movement, the term "culture" tends, in the discourse of the human sciences (ethnography, anthropology, sociology, and so forth), to supersede the earlier term "civilization." The terminological change itself reflects a broad intellectual aspiration to think beyond a traditional Euro-centric model in which "Western civilization" is regarded as exceptional and superior. The term *culture*, in many different kinds of thinkers, seems to promise a nonhierarchical or nonjudgmental term for the customs or ideas of a particular human group, and thus implicitly indicates that *all* human cultures are equally open to analysis, and even equally valuable. This same term, one might argue, aspires to resist anthropocentrism as well, by implying an analogy between the domain of human practice and the cultivation of fields, gardens, and microorganisms (agriculture, horticulture, germiculture, etc.). To take one notable recent example, Sandor Ellix Katz, in his magisterial compendium of *The Art of Fermentation*, discovers a profound significance in this double meaning of the word "culture." Katz argues that microorganisms are quite literally "coevolutionary partners" with humanity, meaning not only that "successful coexistence with microbes in our midst is a biological imperative," but also that the arts of fermentation are, in effect, the condition of possibility for all the rest of culture in the human sense of the word.[10]

Now, as we recall, Pollan also suggests that the ability to bake bread, the ability to transform "a pile of cheap flour and free water" into something nourishing and pleasurable, gave him a new "self-reliance." Here again, one can only agree that knowledge of this vital craft might prove useful in a variety of situations.

And yet, as Pollan acknowledges elsewhere in the same text, to bake bread at home, in real life, also opens up a whole new set of needs and relationships. Unless I am also planning to set up as a farmer and a miller, I will always remain—precisely *as* a baker—multiply dependent on other people and a complexly organized society. Even the water from my tap is not exactly free in every sense of the word, as we Californians are being currently reminded. Trying to bake bread at home has made me newly aware of where the flour I use comes from and under what conditions it was produced. It has also made me conscious of being part of a certain "history" insofar as today's so-called artisanal breads are the ultimate example of what famed Parisian baker Lionel Poilâne calls "retro-innovation": the rediscovery and redeployment on a "quasi-industrial scale" of preindustrial techniques of production.[11]

Let us also notice that, in both of these observations, bread seems to be understood, above all, as embodying a victory over *time*. And, of course, in great many ways it is exactly that. The Apollonian structure of the risen loaf does seem to triumph over what Pollan calls the "living" and "shifting" substance of the dough (except that it also instantly begins to endure the process we call "getting stale"). The experience and process of bread obviously involves the kind of prudence and economy of which grain agriculture has always been the privileged example. In agriculture (citing the first "Satire" of the celebrated Roman poet Horace) we must emulate the "hard-working ant" and be *non incauta futuri*, "not unmindful of the future."[12] (Horace's double negative seems in itself to represent a miniature act of procrastination, as though to acknowledge that human beings must *force* themselves to confront the future.) In his essay "Self-Reliance," one of the supreme philosophic expressions of individuality and independence, Ralph Waldo Emerson understands the problems of finite, mortal existence—the problems of procrastination and prudence, of anticipation and memory—as the consequences of a fall from an original natural innocence:

> These roses under my window make no reference to former roses or to better ones; they are for what they are; they exist with God to-day. There is no time to them. . . . But man postpones or remembers; he does not live in the present, but with reverted eye laments the past, or, heedless of the riches that surround him, stands on tiptoe to foresee the future. He cannot be happy and strong until he too lives with nature in the present, above time.[13]

This aspiration to live in the moment, to be wholly and perfectly self-present, is of course a profoundly seductive one. Nevertheless, I suggest that the experience of bread somehow invites us to think otherwise, precisely in the way, either as object or idea, it disseminates in an immense dance of time and space at once biochemical, historical, and symbolic.

Perhaps this is why the baking of bread seems always to produce emotions that somehow exceed the simple fact of what has happened, much as the action of fermentation itself makes the dough double or even triple in size and magnitude. In a book published improbably in 1942 in the very midst of the world war with its shortages and rationing, the beloved food writer M. F. K. Fisher became one of the first writers to decry mass-produced industrial bread and affirm the pleasures of home baking. "Forget the soggy sterile slices that pop up dourly in three million automatic toasters every morning," she writes,

> and instead cut for yourself, if you will, a slice of bread that you have seen mysteriously rise and redouble and fall and fold under your hands. It will smell better and taste better, than you remembered anything could possibly taste or smell, and it will make you feel, for a time at least, newborn into a better world than this one often seems.[14]

Fisher's elegantly simple summary can be taken as a final hint as to what I am driving at. She envisions not so much triumphing over time but, as it were, *luxuriating* in it. The joy of the bread is a redoubling of time and space: a joy of retrospect and prospect, of birth and rebirth, of recaptured memory and the fugitive promise of a (better) future.

3 BREAD FLOWER

All flesh is as grass and all the glory of man as the flower of grass.

—1 PETER 1:24[1]

On a corner near my house, there is a lot overgrown with weeds and grass gone wild, and whenever I walk by I can't help marveling at their flowering heads, which make them look recognizably like the distant cousins of wheat they are. These too move in their amber waves, each crowned by a tiara of tufts and tiny berries that technically constitute its flower, though they don't look much like what one usually means with this word. All grasses, including wheat, are pollinated by the wind and so don't need colored blossoms and fragrances to attract the attention of pollinating insects—although, of course, these do seem to capture *my* attention. How could one possibly think the chain of causality or relation that runs from these bedraggled little plants to a perfectly crafted loaf of bread?

There is a fascinating passage in John Locke's *Second Treatise of Government*, long considered one of the founding texts of classical liberalism, in which Locke tries to imagine everything that goes into a loaf of bread. He is arguing that the economic value of objects for human beings is wholly determined by the amount of (human) labor invested in them. In making this point, he envisions the loaf of bread as the result of a complex chain of very different kinds of activity:

'tis not barely the Plough-man's Pains, the Reaper's and Thresher's Toil, and the Bakers Sweat, is to be counted unto the *Bread* we eat; the Labour of those who broke the Oxen, who digged and wrought the Iron and Stones, who felled and framed the Timber imployed about the Plough, Mill, Oven, or any other Utensils, which are a vast number, requisite to this Corn, from its being seed to be sown, to its being made Bread, must all be *charged on* the account of *Labour*.

(In Great Britain, the word "corn" traditionally means either grain in general or wheat in particular. The New World grain otherwise called maize was named "Indian corn" by European colonists who immediately recognized it as the staple grain of the Amerindians, different but analogous to their own wheat, barley, and rye.) And Locke goes on:

'Twould be a strange *Catalogue of things, that Industry provided and made use of, about every Loaf of Bread*, before it came to our use, if we could trace them; Iron, Wood, Leather, Bark, Timber, Stone, Bricks, Coals, Lime,

Cloth, Dying-Drugs, Pitch, Tar, Masts, Ropes, and all the Materials made use of in the Ship, that brought any of the Commodities made use of by any of the Workmen, to any part of the Work, all which, 'twould be almost impossible, at least too long, to reckon up.[2]

Locke's strange reckoning of the incalculable number of workers, tools and materials necessary to produce bread is remarkable for many reasons, not least because he excludes the wheat plant from his accounting. For Locke, whatever the wheat plant does, it does not labor, nor is it even quite an *object of* labor. Yet, of course, human beings not only seed, cultivate, harvest, and otherwise process wheat; one might say that the wheat plant itself, in its contemporary form, is itself also a product of human labor. Wheat as a material being has been shaped in fundamental ways by human intervention—at least as much as the human body itself is the evolved product of (its own) labor, marked corporeally and physically by its endless struggle to wrest freedom from necessity.

The evolved stalk or "ear" of domestic wheat, with its elegant braid sometimes ringed with a tufted triangular fringe, is today an immediately recognizable icon or symbol in itself. (The flower of grain is not called an "ear," however, out of any fancied resemblance to the human organ of hearing; rather, these two words descend into modern English from entirely separate roots.) When early human beings first tried to gather the flower and seed of grasses, their first challenge must have been to find a way to avoid losing most of their crop to the wind. As Tom Standage explains, in the wheat plant

> the grains are attached to a central axis known as the rachis. As the wild grains ripen the rachis becomes brittle, so that when touched or blown by the wind it shatters, shattered the grains as seeds. . . . In a small proportion of plants, however, a single genetic mutations means the rachis does not become brittle, even when the seeds ripen. This is called a "tough rachis."

Human beings gathering the grain "are likely to gather a disproportionate number of tough-rachis mutants every year"; if some of these are later allowed to propagate, either accidentally or because they are deliberately planted, then with each passing year "the proportion of tough-rachis mutants will increase."[3] The modern wheat plant, whose seeds are held tightly inside the kernel (something that is a disadvantage to the plant, because it hampers its ability to disseminate its seeds, yet an advantage to human beings trying to harvest the grain in a reliable way), is thus itself a product of human labor. Wheat evolved through a process of quasi-accidental selective breeding carried out by human beings who became intimately involved in the life and evolution of grain plants as soon as they began to gather them, even before they began to sow seeds themselves.

The evolved wheat flower is thus itself a momentous evolutionary achievement, one seemingly recapitulated in certain famous shapes of bread such as the French *epis*, "ears," and the many forms of braided bread such as the Jewish *challah* that are claimed to symbolize the chain of life.[4]

Francis Ponge, the twentieth-century French prose poet, in a poem entitled simply "Bread," writes that inside a loaf,

> *feuilles ou fleurs y sont commes des soeurs siamoises soudees par tous les coude a la fois.*
> (leaves and flowers are soldered together at every joint like Siamese twins.)"[5]

In Ponge's description, it is as though the changing forms of grain and bread through each of their discrete yet interrelated moments of existence recapitulate one another without end.

In fact, the word *flour* (meaning a meal or powder of ground wheat) is just a specific use of the word *flower*. But this is not because all flour comes, strictly speaking, from the flower of the wheat plant. A kernel of wheat comprises the germ (which contains the embryonic plant), the bran (the husk of the wheat kernel, consisting mostly of fiber), and the starchy endosperm. For much of human history, going back at least as far as classical Greece, the best or finest bread has been considered to be that made from flour from which all or nearly all of the germ and bran have been removed. Such flour, which is usually light enough in color to be called "white," has long been considered the "flower" of the wheat in the sense of the best part of it. In English it has often been referred to as "fine white flour," the first adjective doing a double part, conveying both the sense of "superior" *and* the sense of finely ground, the opposite of coarse.

Thus flour is the flower of the grain, the flower of the wheat. In 1541, Sir Thomas Elyot, in *The Castle of Health* (a sort of compendium of medical lore), refers to "bread of fine flower of wheat"—what today we would call "white" bread.[6] As late as 1755, Samuel Johnson, in his famous *Dictionary*, does not record the spelling "flour" at all. Among the senses he records for "flower" are

- "the part of the plant that contains the seeds";
- "the prime, the flourishing part" (as in a phrase such as "the flower of his youth");
- "the edible part of corn, the meal";
- "the most excellent and valuable part of anything."

Interestingly, Johnson also records one sense of the verb "to flower" as being "to ferment," citing a passage where Francis Bacon writes of a vat of fermenting beer that "did flower," meaning that it produced a foam or froth on the top.[7] This sense of the verb is archaic today, but it additionally reminds us that the first dependable source of yeast used by bakers (other than sourdough) came as a byproduct of beer brewing. The yeast most commonly used in baking is known by the scientific name *saccharomyces cerevisiae*—literally "sweet (or 'sweet-making') fungus of beer."

And, by the way, this means that, strictly speaking, the phrase "whole-grain flour" is a contradiction.

The really interesting thing about this, however, is that the flower of the wheat, the white flour, is not necessarily the most excellent and valuable part. A paradox attends the history of bread that has already been often observed and discussed, yet I wonder whether we have yet fully plumbed its mystery. In most periods of human history, bread made from fine white flour leavened with yeast has been regarded as the very best. Compared with bread made from the whole wheat, white bread is more tender and softer in texture (easier to chew), sweeter in taste, and lighter in color. And, above all, it *rises* more readily and with more final volume. When bread rises, the living yeast cells produce bubbles of gas that, when trapped by protein molecules that have bonded together into strong chains and heated in a hot oven, exert force outward to produce the light and lacey structure of the finished bread's interior, which will have pushed out as far as it can within its own self-generated crust. The fibrous bran contained in whole wheat flour tends to cut the strands of gluten and prevent the loaf from achieving this kind of light, risen structure.

Until the Industrial Revolution, white bread was also accordingly more expensive, and usually reserved for the wealthiest classes. Relatively poorer people ate bread made from flour with more of the bran and germ included, or bread made from "lesser" grains such as rye, barley, or even oats (usually reserved for horses), sometimes with the addition of ground beans, lentils, peas, acorns, and so forth. And yet, as is very well known today, it turns out that the stuff we were taking out of wheat to make fine white flour is actually good for human beings, and that white bread is in fact less nutritious than many other alternatives. And so, to summarize very quickly a history that has been fascinatingly documented elsewhere, once the nutritional value of whole-wheat bread becomes generally known, this whole system sometimes reverses itself, so that bread made with "whole wheat" becomes prized, and "white bread" becomes the food of the lower classes.[8] In the early-nineteenth-century United States, for example, Sylvester Graham extolled the value of whole wheat bread as part of a regime claimed to ensure good health (one that included frequent bathing and refraining from alcohol and masturbation). In the 1960s and beyond, whole wheat flour and brown bread would again often be celebrated and preferred, not just for its greater nutritional value but sometimes in grander terms as well. In *The Commune Cookbook*, published in 1972, Crescent Dragonwagon declares, "Baking a loaf of brown bread in this society is revolutionary, if you know why you're doing it."[9] For a brief moment in what we somewhat imprecisely call the Sixties, it seemed, as Michael Pollan aptly summarizes, that "baking and eating brown bread . . . became a political act: a way to express one's solidarity with the world's brown peoples (seriously), and to protest the 'white bread' values of one's parents."[10] Even today, when such notions seem merely quaint or naïve, the phrase "white bread" lingers in our language to mean something like "bland" or "unsophisticated."

The all-too-obvious way in which white and brown bread sometimes change places with one another in terms of their relative status and symbolic power perhaps indicates something about the strange illogic by which material objects serve as signifiers of social class. Pierre Bourdieu has comprehensively analyzed the mechanism of what he calls "distinction," in which social class materializes itself in terms of an elaborate system of "taste," and in which, correspondingly, the acquisition of certain forms of taste constitute what he famously calls "cultural capital." The history of bread presents a strikingly vivid example of this process. On the one hand, the specifically *social* meanings of bread often seem to concentrate themselves, so that bread sometimes becomes a figure of value or life itself ("breadwinner," "taking the bread of his mouth"), or even of Necessity (Kropotkin's "conquest of bread"). On the other hand, bread can also express nuances of class distinction in dizzyingly precise ways.

In first-century Rome, for example, the satirist Juvenal describes a guest at a rich man's table who finds that he is not being served the same food as the master of the house. As Juvenal writes, when you're dining at this house all you are offered is "bread that is hardly breakable, hunks of solid dough that are already mouldy," while "for the master is reserved soft snowy-white bread kneaded from fine flour." And if one should be daring enough to take a piece of that, Juvenal writes,

There'll be someone standing over you to make you put it back: "You impertinent diner! Kindly help yourself from the proper basket and don't forget the colour of your own bread."[11]

It was equally necessary to know the color of one's own bread in more or less every historical period up to the present. In medieval France, it is said that there were different kinds of bread prepared for each distinct rank and sub-rank of the upper classes and their servants: a *pain de coeur*, a bread of the Court, a *pain de chevalier*, a bread of knights, a *pain de valet*, and so forth; and by the fourteenth century bakers in Paris were said to make over thirty different kinds of bread.[12]

In medieval England, similarly, there were a confusing variety of names accorded to white bread alone. The finest was called either *pandemain*, an Anglicization of the post-classical Latin phrase *panis dominicus*, meaning something like "lord's bread"; or *manchet*, a word of obscure derivation that might derive from "crown" in reference to its round shape. Such breads were made from flour that had been carefully "bolted" or sifted to remove most or all of the bran and germ, making it as close to "white" as possible; they were sometimes enriched with milk, butter, or eggs, making them probably something like the modern French *brioche*.[13] These were also probably hard to distinguish from *wastell* (a word related to *gastel*, the source of the modern French word *gâteau*, cake) or *cocket*, both of which seem to have still been relatively refined, white breads. Chaucer in the *Canterbury Tales* describes a character that had a face as "*whit* [white] . . . *as paindemain*"; he also describes the Prioress feeding her dogs with "*milk and wastelbreed* [wastell bread]," which is obviously meant to sound shockingly extravagant.[14]

Finally, there were many browner breads, variously named *ravelled* or *cheat* (both words of obscure derivation). Such breads were made from flour not sifted as often or as carefully, so that they were, in the technical language of modern baking, milled with "a higher level of extraction," using a larger total portion of the wheat kernel. At the very bottom would be "household" or "country" or "common" bread baked from flour that that only incorporated all of the grain kernel but sometimes consisted mostly or even entirely of the remnants from sifting white flour; or a *maslin* or *miscelin* bread (from a root meaning "mixed") made from various grains, seeds, or whatever was available. In hard times, the poor used pretty much anything they could get their hands on to make bread. Over the centuries one reads reports and complaints about bread made not just from mixtures of "lesser grains" like oats, barley, vetch, and sorgum, heavy with the bran and dross sifted from finer flours, but also with the addition of lentils, beans, turnips, potatoes, parsnips, acorns, lupins, wild grasses, and, even worse, ground chalk, sand, bone meal, alum, wood ash, and who knows what else.[15]

In the sixteenth century, William Harrison's *Description of England* distinguishes a bewilderingly complicated spectrum of breads arranged by social status:

> Of bread made of wheat we have sundry sorts daily brought to the table, whereof the first and most excellent is the manchet, which we commonly call white bread, in Latin

primarius panis. . . . The second is the cheat or wheaten bread . . . and out of this is the coarest of the bran . . . taken. The ravelled is a kind of cheat bread also, but it retaineth more of the gross, and less of the pure substance of the wheat; and this, being more slightly wrought up, is used in the halls of the nobility and gentry only. . . . The next sort is named brown bread, of the colour of which we have two sorts: one baked up as it cometh from the mill, so that neither the bran nor the flour are any whit diminished. . . . The other hath little or no flour left therein at all . . . and it is not only the worst and weakest of all the other sorts, but also appointed in old time for servants, slaves, and the inferior kind of people to feed upon. Hereunto likewise, because it is dry and brickle in the working (for it will hardly be made up handsomely into loaves) some add a portion of rye meal . . . and then it is named miscelin, that is, bread made of mingled corn.

The second-to-last bread Harrison mentions, the bread of servants and "inferior people," sounds like it was made virtually from bran alone, with "little or no flour left therein at all." It's not easy to even imagine what this kind of bread would be like. And as if that wasn't bad enough, Harrison once again confirms that, in hard times, some people are "forced to content themselves . . . with bread made either of beans, peas, or oats, or . . . acorns"; adding that "of which scourge the poorest do soonest taste, sith they are least able to provide themselves of better."[16]

Although colorful names such as *pandemain* and *wastel* and *cocket* no longer remain in circulation in modern English, bread obviously remains today an intricately nuanced social signifier. So-called artisanal breads, handmade by skilled craftspeople, are available at exclusive bakeries in major American cities, but for most people they remain a relatively unattainable luxury and therefore a potential indicator of privilege and wealth. Even at the supermarket, in my experience, bread is often sold in at least three different ways: (1) paper-wrapped "artisanal"-style loaves (either baked elsewhere, or else made and frozen elsewhere and then baked on the premises); (2) regular sliced bread, white, brown and various in-betweens, wrapped in plastic bags; and (3) frozen loaves from the freezer case.

Perhaps it is (at least in part) because humanity first began to eat bread as part of a momentous change from a nomadic existence to a sedentary, agricultural one, that it continues to so commonly evoke a thought of the Self and the Other and to locate itself at the very intersection of the material and the symbolic. A range of myths from various human cultures portray bread as a divine gift to humanity, myths that may preserve some distant memory of humanity's shift to a settled agricultural life.[17] In Genesis, for example, it is striking that the first living thing that God creates is "grass" (1:11); and that when God punishes Adam for his sin, even before the famous condemnation to labor, he first condemns humanity to "eat the herb of the field" (3:18).

Such myths, in turn, eventually produce a conventional poetic opposition between corn and wheat as symbols of civilization, and the acorn as a symbol of poverty and pre-civilized nature. In the first of Virgil's *Georgics*, the poet invokes "bounteous Ceres" by whose grace "Earth changed [the] acorn for the rich corn ear," and later praises the goddess as being "the first to teach men to turn the earth with iron, when the acorns . . . of the sacred wood began to fail." Therefore, says the poet, you should all always work hard in your fields, or "you will gaze on your neighbour's large store of grain, and you will be shaking oaks in the woods to assuage your hunger."[18] The Roman satirist Juvenal, similarly, invokes the "country gods" with whose "help and assistance . . . people acquired their distaste for the ancient acorn after their gift of the welcome ear of corn."[19] The same point survives in the form of a familiar English proverb: "Acorns were good until bread was found."[20] Here again, the wheat plant serves as a privileged figure or symbol of the human passage from nature to culture or, in a word, of *progress*.

Just so, the lowly acorn would continue to be associated, in European literature and thought, both with poverty (the proverbial instance of a food which one would turn to only out of desperate need) and with our collective past as hunter-gatherers. (The English word *acorn*, by the way, derives from the Latin *ager*, land or soil, making it a cousin of the modern word "acre"; yet many English speakers and writers over the centuries misunderstand the word as deriving from "oak-corn," meaning the grain produced by the oak tree.) In 1629, as he reached the twilight of his career at the age of fifty-seven, the great English poet and playwright Ben Jonson was deeply wounded by the commercial failure of his play *The New Inne*. He responded by writing an "Ode to Himself" in which, among other things, he denounces the bad artistic taste of his audience. But here is how he puts that point:

> Say that thou pours't them wheat,
> And they will acorns eat;
> 'Twere simple fury still thyself to waste
> On them as have no taste!
> To offer them a surfeit of pure bread,
> Whose appetites are dead!
> No, give them grains their fill,
> Husks, draff to drink and swill.[21]

(The word "grains" here refers to the used, leftover grain from which beer had been made; and such "beer-grains" or "draff" were often used as animal feed, as were the "husks" of wheat kernels.) Jonson's figure may seem rather academic to a modern reader; but it may help us recall its original power to compare a letter written two years later, in France, from the Duke of Orleans to his brother, King Louis XIV, informing him that his subjects "in the countryside, are dying of hunger, while others survive only on acorns, or grass, like animals."[22]

Some half a century later, in Locke's *Second Treatise*, the act of gathering an acorn continues to serve as the model for an alleged natural right to property:

> He that is nourished by the Acorns he pict up under an Oak . . . has certainly appropriated them to himself. No body can deny but the nourishment is his. I ask then, When did they begin to be his? When he digested? Or when he eat? Or when he boiled? Or when he brought them home? Or when he pickt them up? And 'tis plain, if the first gathering made them not his, nothing else could.

"Whatever bread is more worth than acorns," he writes a few pages later, "is wholly owing to labour and industry"; and thus the value of a loaf of bread "must all be charged on the account of labour, and received as an effect of that: nature and the earth furnished only *the almost worthless materials*, as in themselves" (emphases added).[23]

Should we hesitate for a moment over Locke's insistence that the raw materials of the bread are of no worth in themselves? It is perhaps becoming a little more common today to recognize that natural resources, whether of the so-called animate or inanimate kind, are not a simple gift to humanity to be used freely without limit. But even apart from all practical questions about the management of the soil, the water, the air, and so forth (questions that press urgently on humanity today), would it be possible or worthwhile to question Locke in a more general philosophic sense—for example, as a question of what might be called ontology, a question of Being itself? More than one writer in contemporary philosophy has argued for what has been called a "flat" or "tiny" ontology—that is, to summarize only very briefly and simply, the idea that all beings in the universe have a kind of radical equality simply *as* beings.[24] Flat ontology would oppose itself, taking one inevitable example among others, to Plato, in whose philosophy the universe is radically hierarchical, and in particular, divided between "things" and "ideas"—between "the sensible" (that which can be known by the senses) and "the intelligible" (that which be known only by the mind). Today, by contrast, some philosophers are entertaining a kind of radical immanence by which the world would be, so to speak, all in all: no longer divided between things understood as "physical" and things understood as somehow beyond physicality—or "metaphysical."

Correspondingly, many thinkers in the last few decades have sought to trouble the seemingly absolute line between the so-called human and the so-called animal. But ought we extend such a line of thought to plants as well? To cite the titles of two notable recent books, ought we to consider, as Matthew Hall suggests, *Plants as Persons*, and accordingly to think the possibility of what Michael Marder calls *Plant Thinking*?[25] As Marder summarizes, philosophy has commonly disregarded "the ontic exuberance and uncontrollable efflorescence of vegetal life" (all too often seeing both as merely forces to be channeled and exploited); and ignored the possibility that "this life's ontological potentialities" might be "still working themselves out in various guises in animals and human beings."[26]

Could it be, in other words, that plants flower not *for* us but *in* us, as perhaps also we in them?

Unable to answer so difficult a question in even a tentative way, I can do little more here than mark it as remaining to be asked, even at the very frontiers of contemporary thought. For the moment, watching the grasses swaying in their ineffable rhythms, it seems enough to know that, as Luce Irigaray writes, "the plant will have nourished the mind that contemplates the blooming of its flower."[27]

4 BREAD DREAD (1)

Coming into the kitchen in the cool of the morning, I pry open the top of a clear plastic container and peer in. The surface of the cream-colored pudding-like substance in the container is broken by a network of small bubbles that have burst over and around one another, as though trying to climb the sides. "It's alive!" I murmur beneath my breath, in the imagined intonations of Colin Clive as Dr. Frankenstein in James Whale's 1931 film. It's a dumb joke, but I can't help myself. This is what the French call *levain*, and what we call in English leaven, or leavening, or perhaps sourdough "starter" or sourdough "mother," (or, in Great Britain, "barm"); and for some reason working with it always lifts me and fills me with levity. No wonder that, in British English, "barmy" is slang for something like "flighty" or "a little bit crazy."

At the moment, I am especially pleased because a culture or colony of microorganisms has newly taken up residence in my kitchen. Although I am undoubtedly responsible for them being here at the moment, what verb is the right one to express what I did? Another of our great contemporary writers about food, Ken Albala, in *The Lost Art of Real Cooking* (co-authored with Rosanna Nafziger), gives useful instructions for how to "catch some wild yeast."[1] And yet, did I *catch* them . . . or just *invite* them? All I did was put out regular food and water and ensure an ambient temperature and environment otherwise neither better nor worse than my own. I certainly I did not "sow" or "plant" these organisms, though the English language does allow me to write that I "cultured" or "cultivated" them in the sense of preparing an appropriate environment for their propagation. But where did they come from? Some recipes for making sourdough culture call for mixing some flour with a bunch of organic grapes or some raisins, since yeast spores commonly are found on their skins. But this levain, as it happens, came from nothing more than flour, water, and the air of my kitchen. The yeast spores can only have been always already here, in the air, on my skin, in the flour itself, everywhere.

In the levain, some yeast cells have now become active, starting to consume the simple sugars in the flour and producing alcohol and carbon dioxide gas, the latter responsible for the bubbles I can see in the culture itself as well as for the rising of the bread that will be made with it. The bacteria, for their part, are metabolizing more complex sugars than the yeast can, and producing lactic acid, which gives sourdough bread its characteristic tang as well as helping the baked loaf stay fresh. Their twin metabolic activities are tending to make the environment of the culture less hospitable to other microorganisms that might compete for the available nourishment, thus forming a kind of symbiosis.

The verb "to ferment" comes from a root meaning "to boil," and an active sourdough culture does sometimes seem to resemble a boiling liquid. But it is as if the boil has been slowed down or even arrested in time. At any moment one sees only a kind of cratered landscape of broken bubbles, but if one stares at the surface closely for a time you can almost see, or perhaps merely *sense*, that it is pulsing or pulsating very slightly here and there as if it were breathing, not in the rhythmic seesaw of the human breath but in a sort of oceanic surge of multiple swellings and withdrawals. If it gets really active sometimes you can see the bubbles emerging one by one as if from a thermal mud pit.

This levain had been living with me on and off for over a year. Yeast cultures get more active in a warmer environment, so if you keep a levain at room temperature, you have to feed it at least once a day or more. If you cool it down by putting it in the refrigerator, its activity slows, so you can get away with feeding it about once a week or even less. Eventually the yeast becomes entirely dormant, though for a very long time it can be revived by providing food and the right conditions. This one, however, had been neglected in the refrigerator for too long, and so I had been trying to refresh or revive it by feeding it fresh water and flour at regular intervals for several days. I thought I had seen some microbial activity the day before, but it seemed to be taking its time and I was starting to worry that, as the old expression goes, it didn't look like living.

On the day in question, however, the culture was undoubtedly alive and flourishing: the bubbles of carbon dioxide had come so fast and thick that the culture had climbed the walls of the container and was visibly three-dimensional. Frances Ponge, whose prose poem "Bread" I have cited once before, describes the crusty surface of a baked loaf as giving a "panoramic impression . . . as though you held the Alps, the Taurus, or the Cordillera of the Andes in your hand."[2] But the top of the levain is more like the surface of the moon, pockmarked with craters that have welled up mysteriously from *within*.

Many of those who have written about sourdough acknowledge that its thrills and pleasures sometimes coexist with a mild yet inexplicable disquiet. In her introduction to the famous vegetarian cookbook *Laurel's Kitchen* (1976), Carol Flinders describes watching her friend and coauthor Laurel bake bread. The dough, she writes,

> seemed to come alive in her hands . . . [and] was a sort of living entity for her: Laurel thinks of herself as merely an accessory to the whole process whose part it is to call to life the one-celled microorganisms who do all the work. She nurses a warm affection for the tiny creatures—the "yeast beasties," as she calls them—and never feels completely right about the use we put them to.[3]

Writing just a year later, Elizabeth David, in *English Bread and Yeast Cookery*, suggests that yeast is

> mysterious, magical. No matter how familiar its action may become nor how successful the attempts to explain

it in terms of chemistry and to manufacture it by the ton, yeast still to a certain extent retains its mystery.[4]

I suspect such feelings are familiar to most home bakers. For one thing, in order to refresh the levain as I have been doing, each day I had to throw most of it away, replacing it with fresh flour and water. Now that is has become active, I will either have to use most of it to bake a loaf or two of bread (reserving a small amount to feed and keep alive for next time), or else discard most of it yet again before feeding. Especially if you're not baking often, this can quickly start to seem wasteful. And, of course, even if I do bake with it, the yeast cells I have carefully coaxed into existence and then nurtured into furious activity are, let's face it, going to get shoved into a very hot oven where in a few minutes they will all die, leaving behind merely the traces of their presence in the lacey texture of the bread.

But the disquiet that sometimes attends this process of working with a culture of alien beings can also cut in the other direction—since after all, as Aaron Bobrow-Strain writes:

> When I gaze affectionately at jars of *Saccharomyces cerevisiae* imprisoned in my fridge, *Saccharomyces cerevisiae* does not wag its ascospores at me. Sometimes it refuses to help me bake bread when I need to, and I am aware that any ideas of control or conquest I might have are illusions. I negotiate with the invisible world, trying to cultivate an advantageous ecology; but I don't control it.[5]

This is the fulcrum on which the experience of working with levain seems to turn: on the one side, a slight discomfort about working with (or is it even exploiting?) alien beings; on the other side, an awareness that those beings can never be controlled absolutely anyway but only at most channeled or shepherded in certain directions, to the point that it will remain always open to question as to which of us is "using" the other.

For that matter, however, even if I refuse to call it "my" levain and speak only of working *with* it, *who* or *what* am I working with? How could one articulate or define our relationship? Albala, in the same book cited above, explains that he named his levain starter "Durga after the Hindu goddess whose name means 'unfathomable' female principle of unforgiving rage and enduring, endless love."[6] The name seems to capture something essential about the strange otherness of bread, the way it suspends itself between the ferment of creation and the ferment of decay. I confess, a little guiltily, that I spent some time trying to think of an appropriate name for *this* levain, as a though such a name might provide our relationship at last with some kind of fully realized mutuality.

I found, however, that I simply could not bend my mind to think of the levain as either "he" or "she," nor even "they," that I had been reduced to referring to it, as I just did again, as "it." Perhaps I could find no appropriate name for my levain because there simply is no propriety on either side of this situation: just as I do not truly own this levain, so, by the same token, it seems impossible to conceptualize the yeast cells as having a claim on "me." Our relation is exorbitant with regard to any common understanding of property or self-interest.

The phenomenon of yeast fermentation obviously also raised mixed emotions in the ancient human beings who first observed and learned to harness it. Among other things, a rising, leavened dough seems to double or even triple in volume and magnitude, yet this apparent increase is a kind of illusion, since it is merely the visual trace of the bubbles of air pushing their way into the network of protein and starch molecules. Isn't it easy to see how a phenomenon at once so visually dramatic, so potentially deceptive, and so vitally useful—a phenomenon, moreover, whose causes were entirely unknown until the nineteenth century—might raise a certain wariness or suspicion?

On the evidence of the scriptures, the ancient Hebrews certainly knew how to make leavened breads, but there are two scriptural stories indicating that unleavened bread was prepared when a meal was needed in a hurry. In Genesis, when three strangers visit Abraham unexpectedly, he orders his wife Sarah to "make ready quickly three measures of fine meal, knead it, and make cakes upon the hearth" (18:6). Just afterward, two angels pay a surprise visit to Lot in Sodom, and he, similarly, "made them a feast, and did bake unleavened bread" (19:3). Such stories seem to suggest that unleavened bread was consumed only when there wasn't time to make anything better. The same seems to be true of *matzah*, the unleavened bread that supposedly commemorates the bread baked by the children of Israel in haste during their flight from Egypt. The account of this part of the story in Exodus is strikingly specific: on the journey, says the text, "the people took their dough before it was leavened, their kneading troughs being bound up in their clothes upon their shoulders" (Exod. 12:34). Yet in the *Hagadah*, the ancient text used for the *seder*, the ritual celebrating the Passover, one of the first prayers to be recited, declares of the *matzah*:

> This is the bread of affliction
> Which our forefathers ate in the land of Egypt.
> Let all those who are hungry come and eat with us.
> Let all those who are in need come and share our meal.[7]

As has long been noted, this famous passage seems to contradict the other explanation for the symbolism of the *matzah*, which is here said to be *lechem oni*—literally, "bread of distress" or even "bread of poverty" (cf. Deut. 16:3).[8] In other words, what is usually identified as a bread of liberation, marked by the people's haste toward freedom, is here declared to be a bread of enslavement and suffering. And yet, strangely enough, it is this unleavened bread, this bread of poverty and privation, that the text asks us to offer to all who are hungry. Rabbi Jonathan Sacks suggests intriguingly that the double symbolism of the *matzah* is intended to indicate in itself the passage from slavery to freedom, since only a free human being with no fear of present privation has the power to *offer* the gift of bread to another.[9]

Intriguingly, the Torah (the first five books of the Hebrew scriptures) also stipulates that only "unleavened cakes of fine flour" (Lev. 2:4) may ever be presented to God himself as a burnt offering. In fact, the Torah almost always mentions leaven and leavened bread negatively, in the form of prohibitions against their consumption or use, not only during the feast of Passover but in a range of other ritual contexts. One of the only exceptions is the ceremony of the "first fruits" in which, among other offerings, adult men are commanded to offer to the priests two loaves of bread "of fine flour" and "baked with leaven" (Lev. 23:17). The Hebrew word for leaven or leavened bread is *chametz*, which derives from a root meaning "pungent" or "sour" and which could be employed figurally to mean something like "harsh." The speaker of Psalm 71, for example, asks God to "deliver me . . . out of the hand of the unrighteous and cruel [*chametz*] man" (71:4).

But why should the Hebrews have regarded leavened bread in this ambivalent way, as somehow impure? It has been suggested that they associated leavened bread with the Egyptians, who were probably the first people to discover how to bake it, and who, at least in the Hebrews' own legends, had once enslaved them. The centrality of the Passover holiday, otherwise known as the "Feast of Unleavened Bread," within the Jewish ritual calendar, might tend to support such a hypothesis. But the religious suspicion about leavening may also derive, at least in part, from the erotic and sexual associations of bread. As many have suggested, the practical conditions both of agriculture and baking (the furrowing plough, the rising dough, the loaf thrust into a hot oven) offer themselves as obvious potential metaphors for sex. The prophet Hosea, for example, compares "adulterers" to "an oven heated by the baker: who ceaseth from raising after he hath kneaded the dough, until it be leavened" (Hos. 7:4). The word translated as "raising" in the King James Version of this passage has also been translated as "stirring," and is used elsewhere in the scriptures in the sense "to wake." Thus in this context the word probably means something like "to stir up."

Some food historians suggest that loaves of bread in the ancient Middle East were shaped like a phallus, so that the rising of the dough would probably have compounded an association with sex.[10] Bernard Dupaigne documents various later examples of bread baked in sexually suggestive shapes—from the Venetian *pane piave*, little phallic-shaped rolls, to the French *pain fendus* or the Belgian *pistolet*, round or almond shaped loaves slit lengthwise by a deep groove and intended, it is sometimes claimed, to suggest the female genitals.[11] The French word *miche*, meaning a large loaf of bread in the shape of a plump disk, has been used as slang for the buttocks. In English, another word related to bread ("buns") has a similar meaning. And, of course rising dough itself—as it billows and jiggles and swells, and yet communicates to the hand a sort of mysterious muscularity, a hidden force from within—is always irresistibly sensuous, even erotic.

Whether because of such practical and metaphoric associations or simply because fermentation is literally a form of managed contamination, the Hebrews seem to have regarded leavening as a kind of necessary evil, and leavened bread as essentially worldly, sensual, or profane. Leavened bread was a gift *from* God, a gift for which human beings owe thanks to God; and yet something that may not be sacrificed directly *to* God. In the Christian scriptures, similarly, the idea of leaven is often used metaphorically in the sense of a powerful and pervasive force, both positive and negative. In one famous parable Jesus says, "The kingdom of heaven is like unto leaven, which a woman took, and hid in three measures of meal, till the whole was leavened" (Mt. 13:33). In this case leaven seems to figure a positive force of spiritual transformation, though this point has often been debated. But Jesus also, for example, denounces the "leaven of the Pharisees" (Mt. 16:6; Mk 8:15), here clearly using the word to mean a force of evil or corruption. Either way, leaven seems to be envisioned as a contagion or transformative power that rapidly spreads throughout anything to which it is added. In another famous passage, St. Paul writes,

Know ye not that a little leaven leaveneth the whole lump? . . . Therefore let us keep the feast, not with old leaven, neither with the leaven of malice and wickedness, but with the unleavened bread of sincerity and truth.

(1 Cor. 5:6-8)

Since the apostle is, in effect, warning his listeners not to fall back into their bad old pre-Christian ways, leaven here seems to symbolize both a contamination that comes from the outside to transform someone or something; and, in what became a famous phrase, "the old leaven," the surviving traces of the human condition from before its transformative redemption.

Primarily through the influence of these scriptural passages, the word leaven comes to be used in a metaphoric way to mean a bad influence or an infectious evil. For example, the sermonist Thomas Hill, writing in 1648, describes a school as being a place where men "may be either seasoned with good or desperately *leavened* with evil."[12] John Milton, writing the following year, denounces what he calls the "vicious clergy" for their "*levenous* doctrine corrupting the people."[13] This sense also survives outside of its original Christian context. The protagonist of Arthur Machen's *The Hill of Dreams* (1907), deploring some new modern homes he sees being built in the city of London, comments that "there must be a *leaven* working which transformed all to base vulgarity" (emphasis added).[14]

Paul's specific phrase also went into the language in the sense of beliefs or prejudices that survive despite other changes in the person holding them. In the passage itself, Paul was probably referring to the festival of Passover, in which Jews are commanded to ensure their homes are entirely free of even the smallest crumbs of leavened bread—a perfect metaphor for a process of spiritual purification. Yet the phrase would linger in English even after this specific sense had become obscure to many readers. Just as the Puritan side in the English revolution of the seventeenth century was later called (by those sympathetic to it) as "The Good Old Cause," so those more skeptical of Puritanism would dismiss its beliefs with phrases such as "the old leaven of dissent." For example, Willem Sewel, whose well-known history of the Quaker movement was published in English in 1722, writes in his introduction that "the eyes of the most zealous men of those days were yet so much covered with the fogs which then were, and *the prejudice of the old leaven*, that they did not discern all things in a full clearness."[15]

Now, all these negative associations, as we've observed, derive (via the pervasive influence of the scriptures) from ancient human beings who used sourdough leaven to raise and lighten their bread without having any idea how it worked. The process of fermentation, with all of its dramatic visible and sensible effects, remained for countless generations more or less a mystery. And, of course, until the industrial revolution, bread often raised suspicions for another reason—because (as we've briefly observed) bakers sometimes added all sorts of strange and unexpected things to their flour to eke it out, including (at least so it was often claimed) chalk, sand, alum, bone meal, and so forth.

I've already mentioned the strange paradox by which the kinds of bread considered, throughout most of Western history, to be the inferior ones (whole wheat and mixed-grain breads, for instance) turned out to be more nutritious and generally better for human health. In the present context, we can see that the history of bread as a whole has yet another ironic twist. When Louis Pasteur and other scientists in the nineteenth century finally demonstrated conclusively that fermentation is caused by living microorganisms, this revelation, far from extinguishing the potential suspicions that cling to leavened bread, became available as a new source of potential dread and suspicion.

Many scholars have documented how a social and moral panic about public hygiene emerged in the United States at the end of the nineteenth century, powered in part by the rapid rise in immigrant populations and various strains of racist pseudo-science and eugenics prominently discussed at the time. As Bobrow-Strain documents in fascinating detail, the first industrial bread bakers marketed their products quite specifically as more *sanitary* than bread baked in home kitchens or artisan bakeries. A fear of disease germs, in conjunction with misinformation about yeast propagated by misguided reformers among the general public, led to a brief craze in the United States for bread leavened with chemical lighteners instead of yeast.

In 1894, for example, Cyrus Edson, a medical doctor currently serving as the New York Commissioner of Health, published a little essay in *Cosmopolitan* magazine on the "Sanitary Aspects of Bread-Making." To begin with, he urges his readers to remember that bread dough is "an excellent nidus [i.e. medium] for the development of germs of disease as well as for the yeast germs." He helpfully shares his memories of "journeymen bakers, suffering from cutaneous diseases, working the dough in the bread trough with naked hands and arms," and reminds us that "any germs . . . on the hands of the baker . . . are sure to find their way into the dough, and once there, to find all the conditions necessary for subdivision and growth."[16] Thus he recommends using chemical baking powder instead of yeast to lighten bread— one brand in particular (the one made by the company who paid for the article to be published in the "advertising supplement" of the magazine).

To mention just one more example, a man named Eugene Christian, writing with his wife Mollie Griswold Christian in 1904, became one of the first writers to advocate a diet of raw, uncooked food (an idea still very much with us today). The book denounces leavened bread in particular as being fundamentally unhealthy:

> We do not wish to spoil the reader's appetite for fermented bread; but since we are discussing the subject, let us tell the truth about it. Bread rises when infected by the yeast germ, because millions of these little worms have been born and have died, and from their dead and decaying bodies there arises a gas just as it does from the dead body of a hog, or any other animal. This gas being confined in the dough, expands, and the whole mass rises. It is at this particular point that it becomes fit for baking—fit for *human food*. Think of it! It is at this point that it is supposed to be the proper material out of which to make the best quality of flesh and blood.

Christian goes on to cite a supposed expert, one C. E. Miller, who argues that digestion, as it happens in a human's alimentary tract, is entirely different from fermentation:

> The difference between [them] is the difference between taking nutritive material, foods, and converting them into living tissue . . . or taking these nutritive materials, as is done by the yeast germ, and starting them on the way to destruction, putrefaction and death.[17]

Of course these strikingly worded claims are nonsense. The yeast in a rising dough is very much alive, and produces carbon dioxide in its metabolism—so the gas is a consequence of its life, not of its death. Also, as is today much better understood, the biochemical effect of microbial fermentation tends to make most foods, including wheat, *more,* not less digestible by human beings. Both writers also use the word *germ* in a manner as misleading as it is effective. This word is actually a cousin of "germinate," and most of its meanings in English are positive ones: it can mean a source, a beginning, a seed, a seedling, an embryo, and so forth. Thus, for example, the embryonic plant within a wheat kernel is called its "germ." It was only because the word also began to be used in the general sense of a causative agent, especially with regard to disease, that the word germ (in the nineteenth century) came to refer primarily to a bacterium or other microorganism, especially the kind that make us sick.

In retrospect, one might say these and other similar turn-of-the-century fears about "yeast germs" and bread have as much kinship to horror literature as to science. Seen like this, levain is almost literally a case of the *living dead*; and our congress with these yeast and bacteria make all of us into Frankenstein monsters made up of dead parts, our "flesh and blood" literally constituted by the decaying remnants of other beings.

5 BREAD BREAKINGS

On the first page of this book I mentioned how crusty, French-type loaves "sing" when they first come out of the oven. As the spongy interior of each loaf starts to cool, it pulls on the crisp and brittle crust, making it sigh and whisper and crack.

My own experience exemplifies a familiar change in attitude with regard to this *crust* of bread. As a child, like most Americans of my generation, I ate soft, fluffy white bread whose crust was just a browner and slightly thicker version of the rest of the slice. Sometimes you just ate the soft white part and left the crust. It would be a special treat if my mother were to cut the crusts off and make a sort of old-fashioned tea-sandwich in which the peanut-butter or bologna or whatever would be enclosed by neat squares or triangles of a stuff that was entirely white, light, and airy. You could take this white stuff and compress it into a ball if you wanted to; and sometimes, similarly, it would ball up on its own and stick to the roof of your mouth while you were chewing it.

But later, of course, I would join many others of my generation in a near obsession with so-called artisanal or "hearth" breads in which the crust is a crucial part of the whole experience—maybe even the most important part. Such loaves are baked in ovens that communicate their heat directly to the surface of the loaf, so that their entire outside becomes a rich mottled bronze textured with spots of gold. To hold such a loaf in your hand is to be conscious of its two-layered form: the crust is brittle and hard (one could drop the loaf and do no more than crack it), yet the loaf is still surprisingly light, like a stage rock made of paperboard. If you tap this hard surface lightly it resounds slightly like a faint, distant bass drum. With more pressure it will crack and finally break to reveal the explosively light or lacey insides: a tangle or tissue of entwining cream-colored strands, wispy at the edges and yet still with a sort of tensile strength that produces the texture that we name with reference to our own experience with it—"chewy." When you break the crispy and brittle crust of a hearth loaf, you also suddenly understand that one thing that must have recommended bread to ancient human beings as an ideal foodstuff is that its crust serves as a kind of container protecting the more delicate insides and helping them stay fresh for a longer period of time.

One of the most important factors in achieving this crust is the shaping of the loaves. Shaping dough is a bit tricky and, to be frank, I'm not especially good at it; my clumsy fingers don't always manage to execute techniques even when I can visualize them perfectly in my mind's eye. Nevertheless, I simply relish doing it, finding it an experience of almost embarrassing sensuality. A risen dough is fragile and billowy and yet can be stretched in a manner that allows it to hold certain shapes. One of the oldest and most common shapes for a loaf of bread is a simple ball. (In France, this shape is called a *boule*, and a bakery is called a *boulangerie*, which attests to the primacy of this simple shape.) To make one, you take a slightly flattened lump of risen dough and stretch a piece of it outward and then back on itself in each of the four directions, finally turning it over so that you have a rough ball with a seam at the bottom. Eventually you can tighten and further shape this ball with gentle downward movement of your hand. With all of this, you are creating a kind of "skin" on the shaped dough that, when it hits the fire, is going to become that wonderful bronze crust.

Just before it goes in the oven you slash the top once or twice with a sharp knife, deliberately breaking the barrier you have so carefully tried to create. The gas and alcohol from the yeast cell's metabolism are going to need to escape from the loaf as it heats up, and you are trying to lead them out through those slashes. Professional baking ovens are saturated with steam before the loaves go in, because the moisture and intense heat will cause chemical reactions involving the sugars and proteins of the dough, that cause the crust to harden and brown. At home I usually use a covered container so that the loaf's own moisture, as it vaporizes, produces something like the same effect.

The baked loaf, bronzed and speckled with gold, will show you an unmistakable map or emblem of all of your labors of mixing, rising and shaping. It's always an intense moment either of pride or embarrassment. If your loaf was shaped poorly, the intense force erupting out of the dough sometimes goes its own way, imperiously ignoring your slashes and bursting out roughly at some other place. But if you get everything just right, the loaf blooms symmetrically, its crust neatly parting at the assigned places and tightly embracing the loaf otherwise. This is the moment when, if you hold your breath for a moment and lean down your ear, your loaves just might sing for you.

As pleasing as that sound is, however, I cannot hear or even imagine it without also imagining the feel of the bread's crust as it breaks beneath the hand, the knife, or the tooth.

No wonder the expression "breaking bread" is such an ancient and common one. Across many languages, this phrase almost always encompasses a spectrum of related senses. To "break bread" means to eat, to divide, to cut, to distribute, and, especially, to *share*. As we have already observed, to break bread is to be *cum panis*, with bread, and with *companions*. The experience of bread—making it, eating it, and thinking about it—thus opens up the ancient philosophic paradox of the part and the whole, of collection and division. With bread, a *dividing* makes possible *a coming together*, and a *parting* makes possible a *partaking*. This paradox of the part and the whole, something that bread brings to light with peculiar vividness, seems to be inscribed in the ambiguity of certain key words. For example, the English word "share" is both a verb meaning to cut and divide something, an etymological cousin of the verb "to shear," and a noun meaning an individual portion, such as a share of stock. Similarly, the French word *partage* can be used to mean both joining and division—and also *sharing*.

In other words, bread calls to our attention a strange economy by which this object is most whole when it be divided, and most "itself" when it be broken.

The words used for bread in the European languages similarly show the trace of this vexed question of the whole and the part. In the Hebrew scripture, the word *lechem* is the only one ever used to mean "bread"; but it is also used to mean grain or food in general, as well as loaf, piece, bit, or morsel of bread. In Genesis, as a punishment for his sin in the Garden of Eden, God condemns Adam in an unforgettable sentence—"in the sweat of thy face shalt thou eat bread" (3:19)—in which the word *lechem* means something like food or sustenance. The Jewish prayer before a meal praises God "who brings forth [*ha motzi*] bread [*lechem*] from the earth." In the rabbinic tradition, it is viewed as significant that human beings are not asked to thank God over the harvested sheaves of grain but rather, over baked loaves of bread: objects to which both divine and human labor have contributed. The Talmud also records a dispute about whether the verb in the prayer ought to be understood in the past tense (praising God for creation, for having brought forth bread), or in a present tense marking an ongoing process, the bringing forth of bread; or even, perhaps, in a kind of mystical future tense. For it was also assumed that, in the Garden of Eden, bread must have sprouted from the ground or literally grown on trees, not requiring the distance of time and space (between the grain and the loaf, between divine and human creativity) that the words of the prayer both elide and bring daily to the mind of the one who prays. Correspondingly, it was speculated that, after the messiah has come, God would yet again bring forth not merely *grain*, but also *bread* itself, directly from the earth.

In Old English, similarly, the word *hláf* originally meant "bread" in general, and the word *bréad* meant something like piece, bit, fragment, or morsel—of either bread or food. But by around 1200, as the *Oxford English Dictionary* summarizes, "*bread* had quite displaced *hláf* as the name of the substance, leaving to the latter the sense 'loaf' which it has since retained." Similarly, in modern English, the word *bread* is used almost exclusively to refer to the general category; and although it is grammatically possible to refer to "a bread," meaning a single loaf or piece of bread, this usage is unusual and sounds slightly awkward.

Some of the most important passages of the New Testament, of course, involve the act of breaking bread: the loaves and the fishes, the holy supper, the dinner at Emmaus where the risen Jesus appeared to his disciples "in breaking of bread" (Lk. 24:35). In the Catholic liturgy, one of the four phases of the Eucharist is known as *fractio panem*, breaking bread. And Jesus was born in Bethlehem (*beth-lechem*): the house of bread.

The miracle of the loaves, recorded in all four of the gospels, is perhaps the most vivid example of this paradox of collection and division. Jesus asks his disciples to provide food for a multitude who have come to listen to him preach. In Mark, the earliest and most detailed version of the story, the disciples respond, with what sounds like a touch of sarcasm, "Shall we go and buy two hundred pennyworth of bread, and give them to eat?" (Mk 6:37). The opening problem, in other words, pertains to what the classical political economists (such as Adam Smith and David Ricardo) call the "iron law" of economy: there is only so much food (five loaves and two fishes) or food's equivalent, money, and too many mouths to feed. We all know what happens next:

> And when he had taken the five loaves and the two fishes, he looked up to heaven, and blessed, and brake the loaves, and gave them to his disciples to set before them; and the two fishes divided he among them all.
>
> And they did all eat, and were filled.
>
> And they took up twelve baskets full of the fragments, and of the fishes.
>
> **(Mk 6:41-3)**

The detail mentioned in verse 43, about gathering the fragments, appears in all four of the gospel accounts of this miracle. The Greek word translated as "fragments" is a noun drawn from the verb "to break," the same verb used in verse 41 and elsewhere in the expression "breaking bread"; so what is being referred to is, in effect, the "breakings" of the bread. Jesus first transgresses the iron law of economy with an act of miraculous abundance and sharing in which the mere breakings or crumbs of the bread become enough to fill "all"; then he insists on gathering up every last one of those fragments so that, as it is put in the gospel of John, "nothing be lost" (Jn 6:12). The miracle thus ends with an act of prudence seemingly at least slightly at odds with the miracle that precedes it.

We have already glanced at Jesus' parable about the woman who imprudently tried to steal some leaven by hiding it in "three measures of meal, till the whole was leavened" (Mt. 13:33), and Paul's cautionary metaphor about the "little leaven" that lightens the whole loaf. In the first, yeast fermentation figures "the kingdom of heaven" as a sort of irresistible force of spiritual transformation; in the second, by contrast, it figures a contagion by which a single sin corrupts a whole community. In either case, however, the metaphor depends on the strange economy by which a tiny amount of yeast will always disseminate throughout a medium to which it is added, the part transforming the whole in its own image even as it seemingly makes it expand in magnitude and volume. To be sure, there is no real overcoming of the law of scarcity in any of this: the apparent rising of a leavened dough is just air, and the bread's power to nourish and give pleasure will still always be restricted by the amount of flour from which it was made. Still, there seems to me a faint note of the comic in Jesus' parable, whatever its other interpretive possibilities. For, as we've previously observed in part, sourdough culture isn't quite an "object" but a community of living beings that, if it isn't used to raise a loaf of bread, will become itself a new set of mouths you have to feed. If someone were to ask me to give him a little of my sourdough starter, I'd be only too happy to oblige, especially since a single tablespoon or so will be plenty to get a whole new culture going. So isn't there something illogical, even absurd, about dwelling on the theft of an object that, in effect, is already everywhere and everyone's, an object whose very nature and essence is to multiply, to rise, to grow—in a word, *to give*?

Now, in the same epistle in which Paul famously invokes the infectious force of the "little leaven," he also repeatedly brings up this vexed problem of "spiritual things" versus "carnal things" (1 Cor. 9:11). All this seems to culminate in another famous passage that entirely turns on the metaphor of bread breaking:

> The bread which we break, is it not the communion of the body of Christ? For we being many are one bread, and one body: for we are all partakers of that one bread.
>
> **(10:16-7)**

Here again, almost every commentator on this passage suggests both that the Greek original is tricky and that, nevertheless, Paul's point is clear enough. Paul is using the image of the Eucharist, the *fractio panem* in its ritual sense, as a figure for the communion or community of believers in general, once again drawing on the paradox of the part and the whole, of collection and division: the "one bread" that unifies only insofar as it is broken, divided, and shared.

In our own times, philosopher Alain Badiou has gone so far as to claim that Paul should be taken as the exemplar of a radical and potentially *secular* universalism, because of the way, in this text and elsewhere, he refuses to "allow any legal categories to identify the Christian subject," and insists that "slaves, women, people of every profession and nationality" be admitted to the communion.[1] This is not the place to evaluate Badiou's argument in detail. But even with only our titular object in mind, it is hard to forget that every *communion* always potentially implies *exclusion*. Even with regard to the Eucharist itself, as Ralph Waldo Emerson observes in his sermon on the holy supper, "There never has been any unanimity in the understanding of its nature, nor any uniformity in the mode of celebrating it," even including the question of "whether leavened or unleavened bread should be broken."[2] The latter question, indeed, has been and continues to be one of the chief doctrinal points separating the eastern and western Christian churches.

I will thus venture to suggest that the paradox evoked by the experience of bread is not so much Paul's spiritual figure of the many made one (*e pluribus unum*), but rather, more like the reverse: that (to cite Donna Haraway's eloquent formula) "to be one is always to *become with* many."[3] This is, of course, quite literally the case with human beings, whose bodies are filled with the cousins of those one-celled "yeast-beasts" disseminating in every levain. We all carry around a community of microbiota that is essential for our health and survival, one so large that at all times our bodies contain more alien genes than human ones. And by the same token, it is also obviously the case with baking bread, in which we literally cooperate with yeast and bacteria to mutually nourish one another. To be alive is on the one hand to be absolutely subject, day by day without exception, to the iron law of economy; and yet, on the other hand, to also be capable, day by day, of maintaining and sustaining one's self by taking small amounts of matter and metabolizing them into consciousness and energy and life. As Emily Dickinson writes:

A little bread—a crust—a crumb . . .
Can keep the soul alive—

A little leaven, a little bread. A whole loaf, a whole life, a whole history . . .

6 BREAD LINE

. . . a history, however, whose fatal limit remains today what Piero Camporesi calls "the disease of wretchedness," starvation; a history of violence and scarcity, famine and dearth; of the bread riot and the breadline.

1

Give us this day our daily dread.
—LAWRENCE FERLINGHETTI[1]

One of the most famous and familiar stories of the Brothers Grimm begins like this:

At the edge of a great forest, there once lived a poor woodcutter with his wife and two children. The little boy was called Hansel, and the girl was named Gretel. There was never much to eat in their home, and once, during a time of famine, the woodcutter could no longer put bread on the table.[2]

Slightly more literally, the text says of the woodcutter that "he had little to bite and break" (*Er hatte wenig zu beißen und zu brechen*) and that now he even lacked *tägliche Brot*, daily bread.

One might take this scene as representing, with absolute simplicity, an emblematic scene of the history of bread. In fact, the whole story of "Hansel and Gretel" turns on bread: needing it, lacking it, losing it, baking it, scattering it. The poor woodcutter and his heartless wife, with too many mouths to feed, try to get rid of their children by leaving them in the forest. But Hansel outwits them by leaving a trail of little stones so that he and Gretel can follow it back home. The next time, having no stones, he crumbles up the one piece of bread he has and leaves a path of breadcrumbs. But he cannot find them again "because the many thousands of birds flying around in the forest and across the fields had eaten them." So, "they couldn't find their way out of the woods, and they got hungrier and hungrier."[3] Hansel and Gretel are led to a house made of gingerbread; in it lives a witch who, we eventually learn, intends to bake the children in a hot oven instead of a loaf of bread, a fate she ends up receiving herself.

It's easy to forget that the trail of bread *failed* to guide the children home.

2

Piero Camporesi has evoked, perhaps more vividly than anyone else, how bread figures centrally in a European past characterized, in his account, by a kind of radical strangeness. In his remarkable book, *Bread of Dreams*, Camporesi suggests that the poor man's bread of early modern Europe, subject as it was to every kind of adulteration and mixture, including psychotropic seeds such as poppy, hemp, or darnel (rye grass), sometimes caused hallucinations, mental unbalance, and dream-like states in those who ate it—especially when compounded by chronic starvation and malnutrition. This striking claim, however, should not overshadow Camporesi's broader account of how the specter of hunger shaped the very logic of Western thought, among other ways by attacking the "sense of time which in a world of destitution never leads into the future."[4]

Thus my chapter's title has multiple meanings. In its most common sense today, one only a little more than a century old, a breadline means a queue of people waiting to receive charitable assistance. It has also been used to mean something like "poverty line," the level of social and economic welfare that is deemed, at a particular historical moment, to separate the haves from the have-nots. But the phrase might also name the very line between subsistence and starvation, between life and death, that for millions has been, and continued to be, marked and embodied by bread.

Today, as we know only too well, "the threat of hunger's Grim Reaper" continues to lacerate "the most deprived, the least protected and least secure."[5] The line between starvation and survival remains a fragile one for millions, if not billions; and, as a great many have argued, our very institutions of assistance and charity also perpetuate the social relations and indeed, the whole society, in which such radical extremes of wealth and poverty are (still) suffered to coexist.

If there are indeed hidden lives in this ordinary thing, bread, then surely the most absolutely secret of its lives are those of the "dead generations" that weigh "like a nightmare on the brains of the living," these ghosts who will not be appeased (as they are in horror movies) simply by bringing their stories to light.[6]

We can glimpse these hungry ghosts only in their scattered traces, as if following a line of breadcrumbs.

3

In the fourteenth century, there were major "peasant revolts" both in France (the "Jacquerie") and in England (sometimes referred to as the Watt Tyler revolt); both were briefly successful and then brutally suppressed. H. E. Jacob writes that

"Le pain se lève"—this was the watchword of the French peasants. In England it became "The bread will raise!"

when, weary of the fourfold oppression of lord, bishop, king, and townsfolk . . . the English peasant arose to win the right to "knead the dough for himself."[7]

In fact, as modern historians have shown, the term "peasant revolt" is doubly reductive: their participants actually came from a wide spectrum of society and had complex motivations. It does appear, however, that among the rebels' various grievances was the complex feudal structure of obligations by which, among many other things, agricultural laborers were not only compelled to grind their grain in their lord's mill and bake their bread in their lord's oven, but then further compelled to pay fees for doing so.[8]

I am haunted by one incident from the Watt Tyler rebellion, at least as recorded in a much-later account with a memorable title: *The Idol of the Clownes* (1654), a text that tells the story of the much-earlier rebellion against authority as a warning to contemporary Englishmen. As told (or at least imagined) in this text, a group of rebels confront the Abbot of the monastery in the town of St. Albans, intending to destroy the feudal charters on file there (because they believed them to be the legal instruments of their enslavement). Before leaving, they smash some kind of stone monument at the abbey "as a token of victory over the law"; this they

> break into small pieces, and distribute amongst the worthies, as the sacred Bread is given in the *Eucharist*.[9]

This incident seems to have the uncanny illogic of a dream, as though a myriad associations are raised, only to be dizzyingly turned on their head. The broken stones of the law displace the broken bread of the old communion; and one object of commemoration is broken into fragments, only to be re-gathered and redistributed to commemorate anew this very act of breaking. Yet doesn't this audacious gesture threaten to replicate—or at least, shall we say, *symbolize*—the very scarcity (stones for bread) that is always at stake in such conflicts?

4

In the first scene of Shakespeare's *Coriolanus*, a history of conflict about bread is briefly but vividly evoked by condensing two moments of riot and rebellion: one ancient and one that was recent when the play was first performed (around 1608). The play dramatizes an incident from early republican Rome (fifth century BCE), in which the Senate was forced by rioters to distribute free grain to the plebians of the city during a period of dearth, a story Shakespeare learned of primarily from Plutarch's *Lives*. But, as scholars have long suggested, Shakespeare was almost certainly also referencing the so-called Midlands riots of 1607, in which farmers and agricultural workers in rural England protested, among other things, what they alleged was the hoarding of grain by profiteers. As Shakespeare imagines it, his Roman plebians/English Renaissance "peasants" are clear-minded about their situation and its causes:

> What authority surfeits on would relieve us. If they would yield us but the superfluity while it were wholesome, we might guess they relieved us humanely. But they think we are too dear. The leanness that afflicts us, the object of our misery is as an inventory to particularize their abundance; our sufferance is a gain to them. . . . The gods know I speak this in hunger for bread, not in thirst for revenge.
>
> **(1.1.15-23)[10]**

Such a passage already exemplifies what E. P. Thompson calls "the moral economy of the poor." As Thompson and other historians have shown, for centuries a rough popular consensus prevailed to what constituted legitimate practices for the marketing of grain, the milling of grain into flour, and the baking and sale of bread.[11]

Correspondingly, in the so-called bread riots that became increasingly frequent in Europe in the eighteenth century and beyond, rioters often did not simply steal or loot but, instead, forced millers or bakers to sell at what they deemed a "just" or customary price. In one period of disorder in western England in 1766, the sheriff of Gloucestershire described how the rioters

> visited Farmers, Millers, Bakers and Hucksters shops, selling corn, flower, bread, cheese, butter, and bacon, at

their own prices. They returned in general the produce [i.e. the money] to the proprietors or in their absence left the money for them; and behaved with great regularity and decency where they were not opposed.[12]

In the so-called "Flour War" in 1774 in France (a series of related disturbances in Paris and the surrounding area sparked by shortages and rising prices of flour and bread), rioters sometimes pillaged but, as Cynthia A. Bouton summarizes, usually "paid the fixed price established by the crowd or in some cases even left IOUs."[13]

5

Although conflict over the price of bread was a catalyst, if not simply a cause, of the French revolution, Queen Marie Antoinette almost certainly never said, "Let them eat cake." This infamous line appears in Jean-Jacques Rousseau's *Confessions* (first published 1782, though written earlier), where the philosopher recalls how "a great princess, on being told that the peasants [*paysans*] had no bread, replied, 'Then let them eat brioche'" [*Qu'ils mangent de la brioche*].[14] She was referring to one of the standard French breads still baked today, a white bread enriched with butter, milk, and eggs, that probably gives us a rough idea of what the highest quality early modern breads such as *pandemain* were like. It's not quite cake; it's just an expensive kind of bread.

But, more importantly: Why does this one chance remark so stick with us?

We seem to think that the whole *ancien régime* (the French system of church and state that prevailed from the Middle Ages to the Revolution) accidentally summed up its own privilege in a single line, a line that, in any case, read strictly in its own terms, is merely naïve or blind or childish. The princess simply doesn't understand that at issue here is something a bit more serious than what we might call "consumer choice." Thus the line has an unmistakably comic quality—for, as Henri Bergson famously argues in his *Laughter* (1899), it is almost always funny when someone "unwittingly betrays himself" with an "unconscious remark."[15] Just so, this line reveals the old regime to have been a system of such exorbitant privilege as to produce, at its own most intimate heart, an absolute blindness about itself and its Other.

But if this line is a kind of joke, it is a joke gone sour, a joke that causes the princess's mere naivete, within a total structure of relations and events, to read as a cruel, positive *indifference* to the people's desperate lack of bread. Is it possible, then, that when we endlessly recall the imagined remark of an imaginary princess (could the line ever be attributed to a man?), we are secretly flattering or reassuring ourselves that *we* could never be so blind—and thus, in the end, falling prey to a naïveté not unlike the one we attribute to her?

6

In bread riots, often the easiest and most logical targets were millers and bakers, those on the front lines of the marketing and sale of grain and bread.

In ancient Rome, the functions of milling and baking were often united. One relatively well-preserved site in the ruins of Pompeii, for example, is a bakery with grain mills and a large stone oven showing signs of the earthquake that preceded the volcanic explosion.[16] In the Middle Ages, however, these two roles became distinct. Millers were proverbially known as dishonest, no doubt because measurement itself (weighing and pricing the grain and flour) was such an essential part of his trade and because his measurements marked the very line of life and death. As H. E. Jacob writes, "The peoples of the Middle Ages were convinced that every miller stole," and that, however carefully one weighed the grain to be milled, "behind closed doors the miller had taken his share and mixed fine sand into the flour."[17] In the *Canterbury Tales,* Chaucer writes of the miller,

Wel koude he stelen corn and tollen thries—

—that is, translating loosely, "he was a master at stealing grain and triple-charging."[18]

Bakers too were often accused of cheating on the size of loaves or of adulterating their flour with various additives, and they also often took the blame when the price of bread rose in hard times. At the same time, baking has also been proverbially known as among the most painful and laborious of all trades, one that alternates between the back-breaking work of mixing and kneading the dough and the scorching heat of the oven. To compare the three images that follow

FIGURE 1 Clay model of a baker at work, Phoenician (900–800 BCE).

Israel Museum (DAM); Photo credit: Erich Lessing/Art Resource, New York.

FIGURE 2 Joss Amand, *Bakers*, nineteenth century version of a sixteenth century engraving.

From Paul Lacroix et al., *Le Moyen Age et la Renaissance* (Paris, 1849). Photo credit: HIP/Art Resource, New York.

(the first, a Phoenician baker from almost a thousand years BCE, the second a baker in sixteenth-century Switzerland or Germany, the third a baker in nineteenth-century London) is to be struck by the essential similarity of baking over the centuries (See Figures 1, 2 and 3).

FIGURE 3 A baker at work. From *The Book of English Trades* (London, 1823).

Photo credit: HIP/Art Resource, New York.

Bakers also commonly suffered from various craft-related ailments, including baker's asthma (from inhaling flour), baker's eczema (in which the pores of the skin become clogged from yeast spores and flour dust) and baker's knee (a stiffening or contracture of the legs from constant standing and stooping). Steven Laurence Kaplan summarizes the conditions of bakers in the eighteenth and nineteenth centuries like this:

> The air in the bakery was heavy, sometimes thick with flour dust and sometimes suffocatingly humid. When the oven was in use, the heat was overwhelming. . . . Bakers' boys . . . could be seen in shop doorways looking wretched, haggard, and pale, like flour-drenched scarecrows.[19]

As late as 1870, Alexander Dumas writes,

> In Paris today million pounds of bread are sold daily, made during the previous night by those strange, half-naked beings one glimpses through cellar windows, whose wild-seeming cries floating out of those depths always make a painful impression.[20]

In nineteenth-century America, similarly, bakers worked punishing hours under difficult conditions, and made frequent attempts to unionize. A baker's union anthem from Oregon goes:

> Full eighteen hours under the ground, Toiling and making bread!

Shut off from air and light and sound,
Are we alive or dead?[21]

7

Just before the turn of the twentieth century the compound word or phrase "bread line" or "breadline" emerges in American English to mean a queue of people waiting for free food. Originally the phrase was meant literally. The first famous breadline seems to have been in New York city in the 1890s, when the Fleischmann Company, one of the earliest concerns to sell a form of compressed yeast for use by bakers, opened a fashionable bakery café and then, at midnight, gave away the remnants of the day's bread to the destitute. In the depression of 1893–94, it was said that the line at Fleischmann's nightly stretched for blocks.[22] As Donald Pizer has shown, in the early years of the twentieth century, the breadline became a veritable "icon of hard times" in a wide range of popular discourse, and, for the writers and artists of the period, served as an irresistible symbol or image "of the human condition in a modern urban society."[23]

Two prominent American writers of the period, William Dean Howells and Theodore Dreiser, left detailed accounts of Fleischmann's breadline at the turn of the century. Dreiser describes the breadline in a sketch entitled "Curious Shifts of the Poor" (1899) that was later incorporated in revised form into his novel *Sister Carrie* (1900). In Dreiser's novel, the protagonist Hurstwood descends from respectability into desperate poverty, reaching the point where he realizes "I've got to eat or I'll die." One of the last times we see him he "was at the midnight offering of a loaf—waiting patiently," his presence at the breadline obviously representing the bottom limit of his social decline.[24]

Howells's brief and elegantly written 1902 sketch, "The Midnight Platoon," seems, in its own form, to be addressing itself to readers much like its main character: a wealthy and well-meaning young man-about-town who, from the comfort of a cab, observes "the double file of men stretching up one street, and stretching down the other." At first he congratulates himself with a "luxurious content" that he is savvy enough to recognize this strange midnight gathering for what it is. Then he notices

> how still the most of them were. A few of them stepped a little out of the line, and stamped to shake off the cold; but all the rest remained motionless, shrinking into themselves, and closer together. They might have been their own dismal ghosts, they were so still, with no more need of defence from the cold than the dead have.

He briefly considers giving money and rejects the idea, deciding it would be useless: "There was so much hunger, so much cold, that it could not go round." Still, as Howells writes at the end, the young man "wished them well—as well as might be without the sacrifice of his own advantages or superfluities."[25]

By the time of the Great Depression of the 1930s, the word "breadline" had come to be used interchangeably with "soup line" or "soup kitchen," now usually meaning a charitable institution such as a church that served free meals to the hungry. In 1931 there were, according to one estimate, eighty-two breadlines in New York city alone that served an average of 85,000 meals a day.[26] In the same period the urban breadline became a kind of stock image, depicted frequently in paintings, drawings, engravings, woodcuts, and photographs.

Perusing them today, such works elicit the irony of poverty amidst plenty so strongly and so skillfully that the images seem to evoke, perhaps more than anything else, a sense of the impotence of art in the face of the social problems it can neither ignore nor change. Compare, for example, Clare Leighton's *Breadline* to Reginald Marsh's *No One Has Starved*, both from 1932 at the height of the great depression (See Figures 4 and 5).

Leighton's woodcut depicts the breadline with expression-ist exaggeration and obscures the faces of the destitute; Marsh's etching adapts a naturalistic style and seems to individualize each face. Leighton's composition leads the eye deep toward a pronounced vanishing point; Marsh, on the contrary, seems to emphasize the plane and minimize any sense of depth. Yet in both the effect is finally similar. In Leighton, the violence of the perspective seems to inscribe

FIGURE 4 Clare Leighton, *Bread Line*, wood engraving on paper, 1932.

Courtesy of the artist's estate.
Photo credit: Smithsonian Art Museum, Washington, DC/Art Resource, New York.

FIGURE 5 Reginald Marsh, *Bread Line: No One Has Starved*, etching, 1932.

the breadline as an inevitable spatial element in the urban landscape; in Marsh, the line of men seems to curve slightly to the left and back, taking the eye precisely to the point where their faces become indistinguishable.

8

Near the end of his sermon on the mount, Jesus asks: "What man of you, if his son asks him for bread, will give him a stone?" (Mt. 7:9).[27]

During the siege of Paris by Henry IV in 1590, the famine and shortage of bread became so severe that "the poor devised a way of pulverizing slate to make a sort of bread from it."[28]

My own father used to claim that, as a boy in a poor Jewish village in the early-twentieth-century Soviet Union, he mostly lived on a coarse rye bread that would crunch against one's teeth because it contained fine sand that had been added to stretch it out.

7 BREAD DREAD (2)

In the first season finale of Mitchell Hurwitz's beloved television comedy *Arrested Development,* first broadcast on June 6, 2004, the entire Bluth family have started observing the "Atkins diet," an approach to weight loss popular at the time that emphasizes avoiding carbohydrates such as pasta, potatoes, and, of course, every kind of bread. The script manages to include a seemingly endless number of jokes about these sweeping dietary prohibitions. "I want a hamburger and French fries," complains the main character at one point, "but I can't have the bun or the potatoes." Another character asks: Is "macaroni . . . *salad*" still off-limits? By the end, however, the whole family has given up the diet, and in a brief concluding scene are shown devouring toast and jam as the mother says ecstatically, "Oh God, I've missed bread!"[1]

A few pages ago I suggested that "Hansel and Gretel" represents with absolute simplicity a scene emblematic of bread's whole history. One might make a similar point about this episode of *Arrested Development,* except that in this case neither the point nor its representation is simple. We have already encountered the irony or paradox by which for centuries the most privileged of human beings busied themselves (or rather, busied others) in taking most of the nourishment out of their own bread in order to make it "white"; and we have also seen how scientific knowledge about microbial fermentation did not extinguish the suspicion that often attends the experience of bread. Now we have to consider one more inescapable irony: that after millennia in which human beings have desperately struggled for bread and often lacked it, in our own time a significant number of human beings with abundant access to bread nevertheless *deny* it to themselves.

As it happens, the *Arrested Development* episode proved prescient with regard to the Atkins diet. Robert Atkins published the first edition of his *Diet Revolution* in 1976, but it was *Dr. Atkins' New Diet Revolution* in early 2002 that made the approach famous. This book stayed on the best seller lists for much of that year, and by 2004 (the year of the show), according to one study, an astonishing 9 percent of adults in the United States claimed to be following the Atkins diet. A year later, however, that number had dropped to 2.2 percent, and in August 2005 the Atkins Nutritionals company, which marketed packaged food for adherents of the diet, filed for bankruptcy protection.[2] Although the company has since reorganized, Atkins is now only one of a variety of plans that similarly promise enormous results from a few dietary prohibitions and exclusions.

This is not the place to summarize all the details of the various diet plans—"Paleo," "wheat belly," "grain brain," "gluten-free," and so forth—popular at the time of this writing. Whatever their other differences, they all seem to agree that bread is the number one thing to avoid. It should be noted, however, that at issue here are complex debates within the fields of nutrition, anthropology, genetics, and evolutionary biology, questions that cannot even be summarized adequately in a page or two, much less resolved. So let it be clear that, though I have already confessed myself a lover of bread, I'm not trying to talk anyone out of eating, or not eating, anything.

Perhaps, however, we can consider a little more closely the historical or anthropological claims that unite many recent approaches to dieting. First and foremost, it is repeatedly argued that something went profoundly wrong for human beings at the time of the so-called Neolithic revolution about ten thousand years ago, when we moved away from the "hunter-gatherer" way of life and first began to engage systematically in agriculture. Second, whatever problems came in with agriculture were further compounded by the industrialization of food production, which began in the nineteenth century and accelerated in the twentieth.

Now, to begin with, the idea that the history of humanity has certain crucial turning points is hardly a new one. The influential American anthropologist Lewis Henry Morgan, in his *Ancient Society* (1877), understands human history as an evolutionary progress from "savagery" (hunter-gatherer society) through "barbarism" (primitive agricultural society), and finally to "civilization" (the development of the arts, law, politics, and so forth). This schema was also adopted by Friedrich Engels in his 1884 book *The Origins of the Family, Private Property and the State*, which drew on Karl Marx's late researches into Morgan and others. Thus this general way of thinking had been widespread for a century when Alvin Toffler (already a celebrated futurist who had coined the term "future shock") placed a similar schema at the center of his 1980 best seller *The Third Wave*. Toffler again divides history into three parts, this time based on the mode of economic production that predominates: a first wave of agricultural production, a second wave of industrial production, and finally a third wave of "post-industrial" or "super-symbolic" production emerging at the end of the twentieth century.[3]

But, of course, all these are accounts of *progress*. In Morgan, in Marx and Engels, and in a myriad other writers across the social sciences, the transition to a settled agricultural life has commonly been viewed as a fundamentally positive thing, at least in the long term. According to this familiar line of thought, the birth of agriculture made civilization possible in the first place, and the industrial revolution opened up new possibilities of plenitude, global enlightenment, and universal well-being. A mastery of agriculture would thus be an essential step in the long historical process of wresting freedom from necessity.

By contrast, the rather different idea that agriculture is what Jared Diamond calls "the worst mistake in the history of the human race" has emerged in the social sciences only in relatively recent decades.[4] One key early reference point, for example, would be Marshall Sahlin's "The Original Affluent Society" (1968), which used anthropological and archeological data to argue that hunter-gatherers managed to support themselves with relatively little work.[5] As Diamond and others suggest, the evidence does show that, at least in the short term, the first farmers not only worked a lot harder than hunter-gatherers, they also, as Diamond puts it, "gained cheap calories at the cost of poor nutrition." For example, the remains of ancient humans indicate that a dependence on starchy grains led to increasing rates of tooth decay and nutritional deficiencies such as rickets, scurvy, and anemia; it also made communities vulnerable to famine resulting from catastrophic crop failures or drought.[6] Agriculture may also have had even more far-reaching consequences, as Diamond writes:

> Besides malnutrition, starvation, and epidemic diseases, farming helped bring another curse upon humanity: deep class divisions. Hunter-gatherers have little or no stored food, and no concentrated food sources, like an orchard or a herd of cows: they live off the wild plants and animals they obtain each day. Therefore, there can be no kings, no class of social parasites who grow fat on food seized from others. Only in a farming population could a healthy, non-producing elite set itself above the disease-ridden masses.

Thus, as Diamond and others have suggested, agriculture, which *seems* to give human beings greater control of their own lives and fates—allowing them to plan for the future (sowing in order to reap), and creating a surplus production that, in turn, makes possible leisure, the arts, philosophy, religion, and so forth—also, precisely as such, made possible social stratification, class struggle, poverty, the whole sordid history of man against man.

These are thought-provoking arguments about humanity's distant past; but in the numerous manifestos, cookbooks, and "how-to" guides for dieting published in recent years they seem to be both simplified and exaggerated in the name of turning them into a few simple rules for modern life. The basic Paleo argument, for example, was already formulated as far back as 1975 in Walter Voegtlin's little-known and self-published book *The Stone Age Diet*. Human beings, Voegtlin suggests, were "designed to digest" animal fats and protein, which is what we ate as hunter-gatherers during the Paleolithic period.[7] After the birth of agriculture, however, cereal grains became the staple of the human diet. According to Voegtlin, the ten thousand years that have passed since that momentous change has not been enough time for human beings to evolve so as to be able to digest such grains without difficulty. "Man's digestive tract," he declares, "is still that of the carnivore," and we have been mistreating it by forcing ourselves to live on bread. As if all this isn't bad enough, Voegtlin also argues that, in the twentieth century, humanity suffered yet another fatal change for the worse when industrial tycoons . . . drafted plans to mechanize agriculture . . . and to lay the ground work for what is now the second greatest industry of the country: the production and merchandising of food products.

The industrialization of the growing and milling of grains, the development of processed foods, sugary breakfast cereals, soft drinks, and so forth, aggressively marketed with "advertising budgets" whose "size . . . attracted geniuses"—all this, Voegtlin suggests, led us even farther away from the food we were meant to eat. Thus many if not all of "man's physical discomforts and health problems can be traced to his modern, highly scientific, yet faulty diet."[8]

Other more recent advocates of this so-called stone-age diet suggest, similarly, that the history of humanity is punctuated by two changes for the worse: first, the development of agriculture itself and then, thousands of years later, the industrialization of food production. Loren Cordain, one of the best-known contemporary advocates of what has now been renamed the "Paleo diet" (a phrase to which he claims to own the commercial rights), argues that wheat was always bad for us, but that it got even worse with the industrialization of milling:

Formerly (before "progress" brought refined milling technology to bread making), almost all cereal grains either were eaten whole or were so crudely milled that nearly the entire grain—bran, germ, and fiber—remained intact, and flour was much less refined than the kind we buy today.

But doesn't that mean that old-fashioned, stone-ground, or whole-grain flour and bread would be acceptable? No, says Cordain,

> it just means that an extra bad characteristic—a high glycemic index—wasn't incorporated into them yet. That unfortunate addition happened about 130 years ago, when steel roller mills came on the flour-making scene. They smashed all the fiber out of the grains and left the wimpy white, high-glycemic powder most of us think of as flour.[9]

(When he says that white flour has a "high glycemic index," Cordain means that it tends to raise the blood-sugar level.) In this account, therefore, wheat gets doubly vilified in a way, however, that finally puts pressure on the logic of Cordain's argument. If wheat is intrinsically hard to digest and just plain bad for us in general, then isn't the point about modern milling practices more or less irrelevant? Does it even work against Cordain's point, since one must apparently ask whether it is the *processing* of wheat—not wheat itself—that is the problem?

Similarly, John Durant (the subject of a *New York Times* profile on "New Age Cavemen" from 2010) declares in his *Paleo Manifesto* that "genetically speaking, we're all hunter-gatherers," and that "*there is a mismatch between our genes and the lives that we lead today*" (emphases original). Yet when he recounts his adoption of a Paleo diet, the very first thing he mentions is that he "stopped eating industrial foods"; and one of his four basic diet recommendations is to "avoid industrial foods." Again, might it not be the latter change alone that produces the reported benefits? (Durant acknowledges in the book that, before changing his diet, he "ate take-out almost every night."[10]) As it happens, with regard to bread in particular there are real questions to be asked about the difference between traditional breads, made of absolutely nothing more than flour, water, yeast, and salt, and the mass-produced stuff of which the inevitable model is Wonder Bread, the bread everyone loves to hate. In his *Bread Matters* (2009), for example, British artisan baker Andrew Whitley provides sobering, detailed lists of the additives commonly added to commercial breads, including various enzymes that manufacturers are not required even to include on their labels. Whitley speculates that any number of these may actually be responsible for the kinds of symptoms some people blame on gluten or wheat.[11]

In other ways as well, the specific claims about genetics and evolutionary biology on which all these diets depend remain open questions among specialists. For example, Marlene Zuk, in *Paleofantasy*, suggests that "evidence is mounting that numerous human genes have changed over just the last thousand years" and that therefore there has been "plenty of time" for our digestive tracts to evolve since the Neolithic revolution.[12] Biologist Karen Hardy and her team published a widely publicized article just as I was writing these pages that uses "archaeological, anthropological, genetic, physiological and anatomical data to argue that carbohydrate consumption, particularly in the form of starch, was critical for the accelerated expansion of the human brain over the last million years."[13] Whereas it has long been argued that the human mind began to evolve when we first used tools to kill animals and cut meat, this new research suggests that we may not have become fully human, cognitively or socially, until we incorporated carbohydrates into our diet.

Agriculture may also have begun long before the Paleo theorists assume it did. In 2010, researchers at three archeological sites in Italy, Russia, and the Czech republic have reported finding grinding stones and starch grains that are 30,000 years old, concluding that these ancient human beings were already making some kind of flatbread with foraged grains and tubers.[14] In 2015, another team of scientists reported discovering seed grains such as emmer, barley, and oats (seeds that can be determined from their appearance to have been domesticated), along with grinding stones, at a site near the Sea of Galilee, suggesting that the people there were experimenting with farming grain, and making some kind of porridge or bread, as much as 23,000 years ago, much earlier than had previously been believed.[15]

Still, no one is going to be talked out of a diet by highly technical questions of evolutionary biology. At the time of this writing, for example, it has been estimated that as many as one third of Americans are following some form of "gluten-free" diet. But what is gluten, anyway? The late-night host and comedian Jimmy Kimmel did a segment in 2014 in which he asked this simple question to a series of people who maintain a gluten-free diet, not one of whom were able to answer it. Yet the facts about gluten are well known and widely available. Gluten is just a complex protein found in bread and other foods made from wheat and a few other grains. Wheat itself actually contains two other proteins, gliadin and glutenin, which combine to form gluten when wheat flour is stirred, mixed, or kneaded. The agitation caused by mixing causes the gluten molecules to form long chains which, as we've seen, are what make possible the structure of a loaf of leavened bread. Approximately 1 percent of the population suffers from what is known as celiac disease, an autoimmune condition which makes it impossible for their bodies to digest either gluten or its component proteins. Further, in the last decade or so, research has indicated that as many as 6 percent of the population may have an unrelated sensitivity or allergy to wheat in general, though it is not yet certain that gluten is the cause. This means that, to put it simply, there is no evidence that gluten poses any health problems whatsoever for at least 90 percent of the population. And yet, as *Business Insider* magazine reported in 2014, the market for gluten-free products grew more than 40 percent between 2011 and 2013, and is projected to reach sales of 15.6 billion dollars by 2016.[16] The business tycoons and marketers that Voegtlin denounces for industrializing food production have been equally busy fulfilling the self-determined requirements of his and other similar diets.

Along similar lines, consider how John Durant's case for a Paleo diet is explicitly based on the assumption that our hunter-gatherer past was a kind of paradise—or at least, as he puts it, that it "*seemed* like the Garden of Eden" when later humans, those overworked and diseased farmers, looked back to it. Thus the scriptural story of the Fall of Man, of Adam and Eve and the apple, is claimed to preserve in mythic form a fundamental insight about humanity's real history:

> *Life was good. We ate something we shouldn't have. Now life is bad.*[17]

For Durant, in other words, there is a historical truth still legible in the myth. But such arguments can always be reversed: that is, precisely when Durant reduces the myth to truth, he invites us to ask whether the "truths" laid out in his "manifesto" might themselves be merely mythic, matters of faith rather than fact. After all, even if our farmer ancestors did preserve a nostalgic, semi-mythic memory of an earlier and different way of life, and even if they idealized it as a lost paradise (in a manner reflected in our scriptures and myths), does it follow they were remembering their past accurately? For that matter, why are these diets always couched in the overheated rhetoric of a revival meeting? Why is it necessary, in all the diet books and blogs, to record so many examples of what one book calls the "Paleo miracle" in action, so many virtually identical testimonies of someone's astonishingly swift transformation from addiction and obesity to fitness and health?[18]

In other words, it's hard to avoid the conclusion that all these narratives are themselves merely versions of perhaps the most common of all myths: the myth of the golden age, the good old days, the long-ago past in which things were how they should be instead of how they are. Behind all of the "blockbuster diets" of recent years, writes Alan Levinovitz, is "the myth of paradise past"; and behind the appealing new fantasies of "Paleolithic, preagricultural, hard-bodied ancestors who raced playfully through the forest gathering berries and spearing wild boar," we can obviously discern the familiar features of the "noble savage."[19] *Those* were the days; it was bliss in *that* dawn to be alive. And now we've got to get ourselves back to the garden.

As I have signaled with this final allusion, perhaps the ultimate irony is that the aspirations driving such diets are, in the end, somewhat similar to the aspirations that drove the turn to homemade and whole-grain bread in the 1960s, and the so-called artisanal bread revolution of the 1980s and 1990s: here again, a desire to go back, to the traditional bread, the good bread, the real bread. In their different ways, both the hippie bakers of the counterculture and the artisan bakers of a later generation saw themselves above all as making a stand against what Whitley scornfully calls "industrial bread."[20] And as such, the recent history of the trade of baking is itself very commonly understood as what Stephen Laurence Kaplan calls (in his aptly named book *Good Bread is Back*) the "age-old story of a fall and a resurrection."[21]

Should it perhaps give us pause that bread is extolled and demonized alike with the same kind of quasi-religious fervor? But then, bread always seems to be invested with a heavy burden of multiple meanings. As we have just seen, sometimes those meanings cut in opposite directions, and accumulate to the point that they not only obscure the mere object but also determine its social destiny.

8 BREAD/DEAD

The gospel of many recent diet books has been aptly summarized as being "bread, the staff of life, is really the staff of death."[1]

Strangely enough, however, the expression "staff of life" comes to us in the first place only via a complicated double reversal in which the senses of life and death are already comingled. The source of this expression is another difficult passage from the Hebrew scripture. God is addressing the children of Israel to reiterate his commandments and threaten divine retribution—war, disaster and pestilence—if they do not hearken to them. Near the end of the passage, God says:

> And when I have broken the staff of your bread, ten women shall bake your bread in one oven, and they shall deliver you your bread again by weight: and ye shall eat, and not be satisfied.
>
> **(Lev. 26:26)**

The Hebrew is *lechem mattâh*—"bread staff," the second word meaning literally a rod or stick, like a shepherd's staff—which is why so many English translations retain this slightly cryptic phrase. This passage is usually taken as God's threat to cut off the food supply by sending a famine in which no one will have enough. Some interpreters have wondered, however, whether the lines should be read as God threatening to strip bread of its power to nourish.

An otherwise obscure seventeenth-century author, John Penkethman, managed to give a new turn to this striking phrase and in doing so give the English language a new cliché. In 1638, Penkethman published a dull book about the Assize of Bread and Beer: that is, the thirteenth-century English legal code that standardized the weights, measurement, and prices of staple goods, and that stayed in force in some form until the nineteenth century. The book includes some dedicatory verses that close like this:

> Let Butchers, Poulters, Fishmongers contend,
> Each his own Trade in what he can defend; . . .
> Yet no man can deny (to end the strife)
> Bread is worth all, being the Staff of life.[2]

The original phrase, "staff of bread," was already a double metaphor in which "staff" meant something like supply, and "bread" meant, as it often does, food or sustenance. But bread itself can now be metaphorically called the staff of life because, as the most common and widely consumed of all foods, it is the stay or support of life. The staff of bread *is* the staff of life.

But precisely because bread is "worth all" in this sense—as the portion on which the whole depends—bread also, and even in a certain literal sense, *represents* death, is linked to death, stands for or replaces death in the sense of keeping death out or away, keeping death in abeyance; and thus bread always seems to associate itself at some semantic level at once with the life it preserves and the death it forestalls. This link now inescapably speaks in the strange rhyme of *bread* and *dead*, even if only with the fatal authority of chance.

In fact, in a number of the Germanic languages, bread happens to rhyme with dead or death:

Brot/tot (German)
brød/døde (Danish)
brood/dood (Dutch)

A Yiddish proverb I have often encountered reads:

Alts drait zich arum broit un toit.

Everything revolves around bread and death.

In the early twentieth century there was a vogue in London for something called "cockney rhyming slang"—in which, as George Orwell observes in *Down and Out and Paris and London* (1933), "everything was named for something rhyming with it."[3] For example, one said "trouble and strife" to mean "wife," or "Can you Adam and Eve it?" for "Can you believe it?" In cockney slang, either "brown bread" or "loaf of bread" was used to mean "dead."[4] There's an often-cited example in W. H. Auden's and Christopher Isherwood's play *The Dog Beneath the Skin* (1935):

O how I cried when Alice died
The day we were to have wed!
We never had our Roasted Duck
And now she's a Loaf of Bread.[5]

It is sometimes tempting, perhaps, to imagine that we are witnessing here how some fundamental or "root" meaning, across the hundreds and thousands of years of early human culture, somehow sprouted and branched and flowered, and then left the traces of its flowering in a chain of related words and similar sounds: *bread, beer, bake, brew, bit, bite, break, glebe, loaf . . .*

But in fact the association of bread and death seemingly indicated by the rhyme is nothing more than a coincidence. It could not be otherwise because what we call rhyme is precisely a similarity of sound between two words that do not mean the same thing. Two words rhyme because they have the same vowel sound and, if there is one, the same concluding consonant. Pray and day; bread and dead. In this case, the sound does not echo the sense; rather, the chime of the rhyme invites us to entertain a kind of formal link between two entirely different words or ideas. In fact, one fundamental assumption of modern linguistic philosophy is that there is no "natural" connection between a word's sound and its meaning: what we call a word is simply an arbitrary link between an idea and a sound.

Years earlier than the play just cited, Auden had written:

Lovers must pray
Though love be dead:
"Give us this day
Our daily bread."[6]

And years after the play, at about the middle of the twentieth century, Auden writes of a certain insight or truth that remains unspoken or incommunicable, although it may be

revealed to a child in some chance rhyme
Like *will* and *kill*.[7]

Is there something like that, some insight that cannot be articulated otherwise, that is somehow revealed in *this* chance and *this* rhyme: bread and dead?

H. E. Jacob claims that ancient human beings were sensitive to the strange fact that "grain could become bread only by previously being tortured and murdered by those selfsame men it would feed." He cites, among other evidence, a Scandinavian peasant's song about "the sorrow of the rye":

First they cast me into a grave
Then I grew to a stalk, then became an ear
Then they cut me, then ground me,

Baked me in an oven,
And then they ate me as bread.[8]

The famous ballad "John Barleycorn" is based on the same image: three men resolve that "John Barleycorn must die," and then they "ploughed and sowed and harrowed him," "hired men with scythes so sharp/To cut him off at the knee," and finally "ground him between two stones."[9] In this case, however, the grain is going to be used to make beer, not bread; but, as we've already briefly observed, beer brewing and bread baking have always been closely related.

There is thus an ineradicable violence attending the experience of bread that leaves its trace here and there across the tradition. As another proverb or bit of folk poetry reminds us:

It goes in living, it comes out dead;
It goes in dough, it comes out bread.[10]

John Wesley, a founder of Methodism, manages to discover in the lived conditions of grain and bread a figure for the central Christian mystery, writing (in one of his hymns on the holy supper):

In this expressive bread I see
The wheat by man cut down for me,
And beat, and bruised, and ground:
The heavy plagues, and pains, and blows,

Which Jesus suffer'd from His foes,
Are in this emblem found.[11]

There might even seem to be something slightly uncomfortable in the way this passage construes the progress of bread from farm to table in terms of a sacrificial logic more commonly applied to animal or even human life. And yet, as Michael Pollan writes, "All cooking begins with small or large acts of destruction: killing, cutting, chopping, mashing"; and so, "in that sense, a sacrifice is at its very heart."[12]

Peter Reinhart, in a wonderful passage too long to quote in its entirety, describes the process of making bread as one in which "life-giving seeds are combined with water and salt" to make a dough that

> undergoes numerous transformations. . . . But, as dough, it is still unable to fulfill its destiny; for this the yeast and other living organisms must make the ultimate sacrifice, enduring the fiery furnace, passing the thermal death point (the dreaded TDP, as my baking students call it), and in a dramatic, final surge and feeding frenzy, create one last carbonic push while the flour proteins coagulate, the starches gelatinize, and the sugars on the surface caramelize.

And, at the end of this process of violent transformation, Reinhart writes, "It has become a loaf of bread, the iconic staff of life."[13]

9 DAILY BREAD

The weary traveler by midnight who asks for bread is really seeking the dawn.

—MARTIN LUTHER KING JR.

In 1977, Barry Goldensohn described a performance by Peter Schumann's Bread and Puppet Theater of their play *Dead Man Rises*—which they had famously performed during the student occupation of Columbia University in 1968, and which can be seen today on video recreated during the company's fiftieth anniversary season in 2013. Like much of Bread and Puppet's work, the play has minimal dialogue and only the barest suggestion of a narrative. As it begins,

> a small, dim spot of light appears before a gray painted fabric screen. An attendant, barely visible in black robes, kneels at the side. A tall white puppet, the Woman, slowly circles the stage and enters the light. The attendant whispers through a megaphone, and rings a bell to distinguish the "speakers."

As the play proceeds, the Woman goes to the river, finds a dead body, brings the dead body home on the river, lays it in her own bed, and, the next morning, opens the dead man's eyes. The slow, stylized motions of the puppets (who are larger than life and sometimes require assistance from attendants) inevitably give the impression of a ritual, as does the play's central figure of resurrection. And when the performance ends,

> The puppeteers . . . pass through the audience handing out chunks of bread. It is not the usual mush but a dark, heavy bread, made of hand ground rye, not flour, and it requires strong teeth. You sit there in a communal ritual tearing at it murderously.

The echo of the Eucharist, or even of some more primitive sacrificial ritual, could hardly be more obvious; as Goldensohn put it, you feel as though you "are sharing a chaw of the seasonal god."[1]

I can recall taking a warm piece of this bread more than once from Peter Schumann's hand, by the large outdoor oven he built on the farm in Glover, Vermont, which became the theater's home base in 1974.

Schumann has often been asked to explain the centrality of bread to his theater. He has sometimes claimed that it is simply because his family lived on this kind of coarse sourdough rye bread "in the starvation years in Silesia during and after the Second World War" (much as my own father told of living on a similar bread as a child in the early-twentieth-century Soviet Union).[2] In a brief essay from 1970, however, Schumann is more specific:

> We sometimes give you a piece of bread along with the puppet show because our bread and theatre belong together. For a long time the theatre arts have been separated from the stomach. Theatre was entertainment. Entertainment was meant for the skin. Bread was meant for the stomach. The old rites of baking and eating, and offering bread were forgotten. The bread became mush.

By contrast, in our show, Schumann suggests, "The bread shall remind you of the sacrament of eating."[3]

By now, this theme of retrospect and renewal should seem familiar, for we have encountered it repeatedly in tracing the thought of bread. But what can Schumann mean with this enigmatic final reference to a sacrament of eating? One could always read this line in a traditional register of faith, since it has long been argued that (in the words of Bishop William R. Inge, a twentieth-century Anglican theologian), "those who, 'whether they eat, or drink, or whatever they do,' do all to the glory of God, may be said to turn the commonest acts into sacraments."[4] But Schumann seems, on the contrary, to invite us to discover or recognize in eating (the very figure of bodily need and thus of the worldly, secular, or profane) a kind of sacredness or holiness—a sacredness, moreover, which has always been familiar to us, and of which we need only be *re*-minded.

Elsewhere, in a "fiddle lecture" called "The Old Art of Puppetry in the New World Order," Schumann writes of how puppets themselves—made of garbage and trash, mere scraps of cloth, wood, and paper—give us what he strikingly calls a "solidarity" with the material world, a world

> which our Judeo-Christian morality has taught us to regard as our property, a world in which we will eventually have the honor to participate either as worms or as ashes.[5]

And as puppets remind us of our origins in the otherness of the material, so bread reminds us, Schumann writes, of the sacrament of eating. The very name of this theater, especially because their work often features a secularized religious imagery, seems to be a parody or comic recasting of the theological and metaphysical opposition of flesh and spirit, the material and the spiritual. This name seems to reverse and empty out this metaphysical opposition, which has either become material on both sides (bread or puppet), or else, since puppets can only be associated with the material, puts *bread* somewhat paradoxically into the place of the spiritual.

If Schumann, too, has been marked to some extent with a familiar nostalgia for a lost past, one must not forget that what he actually aspires to recreate or re-present are "the old rites of baking and eating, and offering bread." Indeed, at the end of Susan Bettmann's film *Bread* (2013), a documentary focusing primarily on Schumann as a lifelong baker, he confides something extraordinary:

> The theater is just a vehicle for the bread, it's not the other way around. There has to be a method of distributing the bread. If you have free bread . . . it's very suspicious to Americans. . . . So in order to do that you have to trick them. This trick is called puppetry.[6]

He says it with a twinkle in his eye and one supposes at first it must be another joke. As he obviously recognizes, we would more commonly think that it would be the theater—the art— that counts the most. The bread would seem to be just a little something extra, or at most a kind of necessary foundation (like the so-called economic "base" in Marxist cultural theory, on which rises a "superstructure" of art, philosophy, religion, and so forth). For that matter, as we already know quite well, even Americans will, in fact, if they are desperate enough, line up to accept free bread. If anything, then, Schumann must be talking about getting relatively comfortable people, people who do not currently suffer from real privation or need, to accept free bread. His gesture is thus precisely *not* the old religious impulse of "afflicting the comfortable." Rather, the distributing of the bread seems to hold out—and, so to speak, even or especially to the comfortable—the living image of an unending plenitude, a truly *daily* bread.

This is one more vivid example of how bread, as object and idea, so often locates itself (citing Kaplan) "at the crossroads between the material and the symbolic," so that it always "forges complex links between the sacred and the profane."[7] This must be why our attempt to trace the hidden life of bread has so often brought us to the threshold of the religious, and why so many of those who write about bread do so with a language of magic and miracle. For example, Chef Alain Sailhac, the dean of the French Culinary Institute, is said to regard "the breaking of bread as a mystical experience" and seeks to instill in his students a "sacramental regard for bread."[8] Peter Reinhart, who has written eloquently and often of the connection between his Christian faith and the craft of bread baking, writes that "most of the serious bread makers I have met seem to be deeply spiritual even if they are not particularly religious," and says that, for students of baking, "feeling dough is really where the magic begins."[9] Even the very word *religion* itself seems to descend into the modern European languages (though its etymology has been long disputed) either from the Latin *religare*, to gather, to harvest, or *relegere*, to tie, to bind, both verbs drawn from or related to grain agriculture. Accordingly, in the whole Judeo-Christian tradition, probably the two most famous and familiar sayings about bread both pertain to the difficult line between a literal or material value, and a transcendent or "spiritual" value. (I put the latter word in quotation marks as a precaution because we're trying to avoid simply thinking *within* the metaphysical schema at issue here by considering it, as it were, at arm's length.)

The first of these two famous sayings also provides a link between the Hebrew and Christian scriptures, the so-called Old and New Testaments. When Satan confronts Jesus as he is fasting in the wilderness, he first tempts Jesus to use his divine power to overcome the iron law of scarcity. "If thou be the Son of God," Satan says, "command that these stones be made bread." Jesus ingeniously deflects him by quoting the Hebrew scripture, where

> It is written, Man shall not live by bread alone, but by every word that proceedeth out of the mouth of God.
>
> **(Mt. 4:4)**

Jesus is indirectly alluding to the story (recounted both in Exodus and Numbers) of the miraculous *manna* with which God fed the children of Israel in the wilderness. As told in Exodus, the people begin murmuring against Moses, accusing him of bringing them from slavery merely to die of hunger, and looking back nostalgically to Egypt where they "sat by the flesh pots" and "did eat bread to the full" (16:3). In the evening, however, "quails came up," and in the morning "there lay a small round thing, as small as the hoar frost on the ground" (16:13-4), which they gather and eat. It was, the text says, "like coriander seed, white, and the taste was like wafers made with honey" (16:31). In Numbers, it is said that "the people . . . gathered [the *manna*], and ground it in mills, or beat it in a mortar, and baked it in pans, and made cakes of it" (11:8). No one has ever been certain what manna really is (if indeed the story itself has any historical accuracy); but the text suggests the people handle it as they would seed or grain, and think of it as a substitute for bread.

Then, in Deuteronomy, in a moment of retrospect, the Hebrews are reminded that God

> suffered thee to hunger, and fed thee with manna. Which thou knewest not, neither did thy fathers know; that he might make thee know that man doth not live by bread only, but by every *word* that proceedeth out of the mouth of the Lord doth man live.
>
> **(Deut. 8:3, emphasis original)**

In this one case I've retained the italics on *word* as they appear in many editions of the King James Bible, to indicate that this word does not actually appear in the Hebrew original but has been added by the translators. The Hebrew word translated as "every" can also be used as a noun meaning "whole," so the lesson imparted by this passage, the thing we are advised to learn from the miracle, might conceivably be paraphrased as: remember that you do not live by bread alone but by the *whole*, by *all*, or by *every-thing*.

There is thus a potential strangeness in this famous passage about living by bread that the translation at least partially obscures, and that has entirely vanished by the time Jesus makes his witty riposte to the Prince of Darkness.

In English, we now hear a clear opposition between *bread* and *the word*; so the passage marks the line between pure subsistence and survival (living by bread), and the whole realm of spiritual or sacred value that goes beyond mere sustenance. But, after all, the event that originally provoked this famous dictum had been a thoroughly material miracle, a miracle of food; so in some sense it affirms a solidarity with, or openness to, the material world not entirely unlike the one that Schumann discovers in the puppet. Without too much of a stretch, we might even understand the passage as affirming, above all, an *openness*—to the future, to the things our fathers never knew, to whatever or whomever might still be to come. For all the people's murmurings, Moses knew, at least, that they could only go further, that there was no going back.

A similar ambiguity haunts the famous line from the Lord's Prayer, whose familiar English translation—"Give us this day our daily bread" (Mt. 6:11; Lk. 11:3)—once again obscures an intriguing problem in its original Greek text.[10] This elegant piece of English rhetoric can be attributed to William Tyndale, whose early-sixteenth-century translation of the Bible (first published in 1526) led to his execution for heresy even as it profoundly influenced the later King James Version and, through it, the whole canon of English literature, for which Tyndale is thus probably the single greatest unsung hero. In this passage, however, the Greek adjective Tyndale translates as "daily" (*epiousios*, a derivation of the preposition *epi*) is an unusual word that appears nowhere else in the scriptures except in the two versions of the Lord's Prayer. The word might mean something like "necessary" or "needful," or perhaps "continual." But because the word is so unusual, some early translators thought Jesus must have used it in some special sense. In Saint Jerome's important Latin translation of the Bible from the fourth century (the so-called *Vulgate*), the adjective in Luke is given as *cotidianum* (a late Latin version of *quotidianum*, "daily") but the adjective in Matthew is given as *supersubstantialem*. The Douai-Rheims Bible (the English translation first used by the Roman Catholic Church), trying to follow Jerome, gives the line in Matthew as

Give us this day our supersubstantial bread.[11]

By contrast, Tyndale seems to be responsible for the elegant alliteration ("give us this *day* our *daily* bread") that serves as the very fulcrum of the prayer as most English speakers hear it today. This phrase beautifully unifies the two related but distinct ideas that are obviously at stake in the prayer, if not in all prayers: the *needful* and the *continual*.

But why did Jerome translate the same word two different ways, and what determined his strange choice of word for the passage in Matthew? A full answer would require a technical discussion of Greek grammar that is far beyond my expertise (and perhaps my readers' interest as well). But it seems clear, at least, that Jerome wasn't quite content with the translation *daily;* and that he must have heard a special sense in the adjective that made him split the difference between the two translated passages. The word *supersubstantial* would be used later in philosophy and theology to denote that which transcends, goes above or beyond, all substance or being: that is, chiefly, God. Taken like this, therefore, the prayer does not simply ask for daily sustenance but for bread beyond bread, for spiritual nourishment that transcends that of the body. And yet, here is the strange thing: even if one throws out Jerome's second translation and insists on "daily"—insists, that is, on the materiality of the prayer, and that it really is about bread, about sustenance—then it would still be asking God for a *double* gift: for bread both today *and* tomorrow. And tomorrow and tomorrow and tomorrow, to the last syllable of recorded time.

One way or the other, therefore, there seems to be a spectrum of meaning at work in this crucial adjective that is too large to be encompassed in a single word. At one and the same time, the prayer declares our finitude in time and space (our *continual* neediness), dreams of an inexhaustible plenitude by which those daily needs might be daily answered, and implicitly affirms, one more time, that there must be something *beyond* this sustenance for which it asks, something *beyond* mere survival, mere "getting-by." In other words, the prayer finally goes in both directions: it confronts the necessity of daily bread without qualification or compromise, and yet (thousands of years before a successful textile strike in Lawrence, Massachusetts, in 1912 gave the world another famous phrase) it also affirms, at least implicitly, that

> Our lives shall not be sweated from birth until life closes;
> Hearts starve as well as bodies; give us bread, but give us
> roses![12]

Here again, bread seems to mark the line where our *limits* as finite beings—our eternal neediness, our finitude in time and space—become the condition of possibility for everything else, for life, experience, meaning . . . and even what we might dare to call justice.

*

Is there anything else to say? Anything and everything, as remains always the case at the end of every book. I confess, however, I found it especially difficult to find a way to end *this* book. And eventually I decided that it must be because there was an essential unfinished-ness about my subject which, as we have seen again and again, is always in process and therefore never one but always many: flower to grain to flour to dough to loaf to slice to crumb.

For a week or more, not finding a way to finish—what else?—I baked bread.

And yesterday, when I came into my kitchen first thing in the morning, I noticed that the container holding my levain or sourdough starter was uncovered. I started to scold myself for having apparently left it that way. The aromas of fermentation can attract insects, and if there were flies in it (it happened to me once!) I would have to throw the whole thing away and start over. Then I noticed that the lid was all the way on the other side of the kitchen; and that the floor and the counter were lightly dappled with spidery lines of dried dough like an abstract expressionist painting. So I realized what had happened: the yeast culture had at some point during the night gotten very active and produced enough carbon dioxide gas that it had literally blown its top, flipped its lid, disseminated itself all over my kitchen.

How can I resist finding, in this small misadventure, an irresistible figure for the way the myriad meanings of bread explode and proliferate and effervesce without end—and even, further, finding *in* that very process of dissemination a mirror or instance of the endless dance of being as it traces itself in time and space? Perhaps this is why bread, as object or idea, is so often experienced as somehow sacred or magical or miraculous: because we simply cannot help but taste in it, day by day by day, the explosive promise of the *plural*, the exhilarating undecidability of *more*.

ACKNOWLEDGMENTS

Thanks especially to Christopher Schaberg and Ian Bogost, the series editors of *Object Lessons*, and to Haaris Naqvi, Mary Al-Sayed, and their colleagues at Bloomsbury. Thanks to Elizabeth Miller and Matthew Stratton, whose children Ambrose and Giacomo inspired me with their "bread dance"; and to my colleague Hsuan Hsu for sharing with me the manuscript of his forthcoming critique of the "Paleo" worldview. Thanks to Gerhard Richter for helping with the Grimm Brothers' German.

A special thanks to Miyuki Togi, my instructor at the San Francisco Baking Institute, whose skill inspires me every time I bake.

Lastly, as always, thanks to Frances E. Dolan: for tolerating all that dough and flour everywhere, for shaping the book in innumerable ways with her comments and suggestions, and, especially (to appropriate words both of hers and another), for sharing with me the wonders of the domestic resurrection circus.

NOTES

Chapter 1

1 David Bowie, composer and performer, "Loving the Alien," *Tonight* (EMI records, 1984).

2 See Peter Reinhart, *Brother Juniper's Bread Book: Slow Rise as Method and Metaphor* (Philadelphia: Running Press, 2005), 26–30.

3 James Beard, *Beard on Bread* (1973; rpt. New York: Alfred A. Knopf, 1984). There are too many excellent recent books about baking bread to list them all. Among my favorites are: anything by Peter Reinhart—I've baked especially from *The Bread Baker's Apprentice: Mastering the Art of Extraordinary Bread* (Berkeley, CA: Ten Speed Press, 2001) and *Artisan Breads Everyday* (Berkeley, CA: Ten Speed Press, 2009); Chad Robertson, *Tartine Bread* (San Francisco: Chronicle Books, 2010) and *Tartine Bread III* (San Francisco: Chronicle Books, 2013); Jeffrey Hamelman, *Bread: A Baker's Book of Techniques and Recipes,* 2nd edn (Hoboken, NJ: Wiley, 2013); and Andrew Whitley, *Bread Matters: The State of Modern Bread and a Definitive Guide to Baking Your Own* (Kansas City, KS: Andrews McMeel, 2009).

4 Karl Marx, *Capital I*, trans. Ben Fowkes (Middlesex, UK: Penguin, 1976), 163.

5 Piero Camporesi, *Bread of Dreams*, trans. David Gentilcore (Chicago: University of Chicago Press, 1989), 17.

6 Peter Kropotkin, *The Conquest of Bread and Other Writings*, ed. Marshall Shatz (Cambridge: Cambridge University Press, 1995), 54.

7 Kropotkin, *Conquest of Bread*, 54.

8 Ian Bogost, *Alien Phenomenology, or What It's Like to Be a Thing* (Minneapolis, MN: University of Minneapolis Press, 2012), 32–34.

9 Timothy Morton, *The Ecological Thought* (Cambridge, MA: Harvard University Press, 2010), 38–50; "Here Comes Everything: The Promise of Object-Oriented Ontology," *Qui Parle* 19, no. 2 (2011): 165–66.

10 Jacques Derrida, "Structure, Sign and Play in the Discourse of the Human Sciences," trans. Alan Bass, *Writing and Difference* (Chicago: University of Chicago Press, 1978), 284.

11 Maria Bamford, performer and writer, *The Burning Bridges Tour* (Minneapolis, MN: Standup Records, 2003).

12 I am not the first to do so: Michael Pollan, in *Cooked: A Natural History of Transformation* (New York: Penguin, 2013), writes of being unprepared "for the erotics of leavened, shaped dough" (232).

13 Frances E. Dolan, *Dangerous Familiars: Representations of Domestic Crime in England, 1550–1700* (Ithaca, NY: Cornell University Press, 1994).

14 Donna Haraway, *When Species Meet* (Minneapolis, MN: University of Minnesota Press, 2008).

15 Reinhart, *The Bread Baker's Apprentice*, 49.

16 For "dissemination" see Jacques Derrida, "Signature, Event, Context," in *Margins of Philosophy,* trans. Alan Bass (Chicago: University of Chicago Press, 1982), 307–30; and *Dissemination,* trans. Barbara Johnson (Chicago: University of Chicago Press, 1981).

17 Marion Nestle, *What To Eat* (New York: Norton, 2006), 484, citing a remark of Mark Furstenberg of Bread Line Bakery in Washington, DC.

18 Thomas Blount, *Glossographia: Or A Dictionary* (London, 1656).

Chapter 2

1 Lisa Bramen, "Breaking Bread (and Dancing With It) at a Macedonian Wedding," *Smithsonian.com*, September 14, 2010, accessed September 2, 2015, http://www.smithsonianmag.com/arts-culture/breaking-bread-and-dancing-with-it-at-a-macedonian-wedding-99451635/?no-ist; Blue Clark, *Indian Tribes of Oklahoma: A Guide* (Norman, OK: University of Oklahoma Press, 2009), 351.

2 Pollan, *Cooked*, 247–48.

3 Ibid., 248–49.

4 Unless otherwise identified, all etymologies are cited from the *Oxford English Dictionary*.

5 H. E. Jacob, *Six Thousand Years of Bread: Its Holy and Unholy History*, Seventieth Anniversary Edition (New York: Skyhorse, 2014), 157.

6 Pollan, *Cooked*, 250.

7 Immanuel Kant, *Critique of the Power of Judgment*, trans. Paul Buyer and Eric Matthews (Cambridge: Cambridge University Press, 2000), 91–98.

8 Sophocles, *Antigone*, trans. Richard Emil Braun (Oxford: Oxford University Press, 1993), ll. 1294–98.

9 Hugh Bowden, *Mystery Cults of the Ancient World* (Princeton and London: Princeton University Press, 2010), 43, 109.

10 Sandor Ellix Katz, *The Art of Fermentation* (White River Junction, VT: Chelsea Green, 2012), 1–6 and *passim*; the quoted line is on page 6.

11 Steven Laurence Kaplan, *Good Bread Is Back: A Contemporary History of French Bread, The Way It Is Made, and the People Who Make It,* trans. Catherine Porter (Durham, NC: Duke University Press, 2006), 8.

12 Horace, *Satires. Epistles. The Art of Poetry,* trans. H. Rushton Fairclough, Loeb Classical Library (Cambridge, MA: Harvard University Press, 1926), Satire 1.1, line 35.

13 Ralph Waldo Emerson, "Self-Reliance," in *Emerson's Poetry and Prose*, ed. Joel Porte and Saundra Morris (New York: Norton, 2001), 128–29.

14 M. F. K. Fisher, *The Art of Eating*, 50th Anniversary Edition (New York: Houghton Mifflin Harcourt, 2004), 251.

Chapter 3

1 All citations from the scriptures are, unless otherwise identified, from *The Bible: Authorized King James Version*, ed. Robert Carroll and Stephen Prickett (Oxford: Oxford University Press, 1997), italics omitted.

2 John Locke, *Two Treatises of Government,* ed. Peter Laslett, 2nd edn (Cambridge: Cambridge University Press, 1970), 298.

3 Tom Standage, *An Edible History of Humanity* (New York: Walker, 2009), 8–9; see also Maguelonne Toussaint-Samat, *A History of Food,* expanded edition, trans. Anthea Bell (Malden, MA: Wiley-Blackwell, 2009), 115; and Leslie Head et al., *Ingrained: A Human Bio-Geography of Wheat* (Farnham, England: Ashgate, 2012), 41–43.

4 Bernard Dupaigne, *The History of Bread*, trans. Antonio and Sylvie Roder (New York: Harry N. Abrams, 1999), 219.

5 Francis Ponge, "Le Pain/Bread," in *Selected Poems*, trans. Margaret Guiton, John Montague and C. L. Williams, ed. Margaret Guiton (Winston-Salem, NC: Wake Forest University Press, 2012), 34.

6 Sir Thomas Elyot, *The Castel of Health*, 2nd edn (London, 1561), 2:28.

7 Samuel Johnson, *A Dictionary of the English Language* (London, 1755), entry for "flower."

8 Pollan, *Cooked*, 255–66; Aaron Bobrow-Strain, *White Bread: A Social History of the Store-Bought Loaf* (Boston: Beacon Press, 2010).

9 Crescent Dragonwagon, *The Commune Cookbook* (New York: Simon & Schuster, 1971), 129.

10 Pollan, *Cooked*, 263.

11 Juvenal, *Juvenal and Persius,* trans. Susanna Morton Braund, Loeb Classical Library (Cambridge, MA: Harvard University Press, 2004), 221.

12 Judith Choate and the French Culinary Institute, *The Fundamental Techniques of Classic Bread Baking* (New York: Stewart Tabori & Chang, 2011), 8–9.

13 Elizabeth David, *English Bread and Yeast Cookery*, New American Edition (Newton, MA: Biscuit Books, 1994), 328–32.

14 Geoffrey Chaucer, "The Tale of Sir Topas," 14, "General Prologue," 147, from *The Canterbury Tales,* in *Chaucer's Poetry,* ed. E. T. Donaldson (New York: Ronald Press, 1958), 10, 351.

15 John Marchant, Bryan Reuben, and Joan Alock, *Bread: A Slice of History* (Stroud, Gloucester: History Press, 2008), 74–76; Comporesi, *Bread of Dreams,* 111; Bobrow-Strain, *White Bread,* 38.

16 William Harrison, *A Description of England* (1577), in *Chronicle and Romance,* The Harvard Classics 38, ed. Charles W. Eliot (Cambridge, MA: Harvard University Press, 1910), 294–96, adding a missing colon after "sorts" in the first cited passage.

17 Standage, *An Edible History,* 15.

18 Virgil, *Eclogues, Georgics, Aeneid: Books 1–6,* Loeb Classical Library, rev. edn (Cambridge, MA: Cambridge University Press, 1999), 99, 109.

19 Juvenal, *Satire 14,* in *Juvenal and Persius,* ed. Braund, 473.

20 *The Oxford Dictionary of English Proverbs,* 3rd edn, rev. F. P. Wilson (Oxford: Clarendon Press, 1970), 3.

21 Ben Jonson, "Ode to Himself," in *Seventeenth-Century British Poetry,* ed. John P. Rumrich and Gregory Chaplin (New York: Norton, 2006), 151–52.

22 Dupaigne, *History of Bread,* 40.

23 Locke, *Two Treatises,* 288, 297, 298, original italics removed.

24 See, for example, Bogost, 11–19.

25 Matthew Hall, *Plants as Persons: A Philosophical Botany* (Albany, NY: State University of New York Press, 2011);

Michael Marder, *Plant-Thinking: A Philosophy of Vegetal Life* (New York: Columbia University Press, 2013).

26 Marder, *Plant-Thinking*, 12.

27 Luce Irigaray, *Elemental Passions*, trans. Joanne Collie and Judith Still (London: Athlone Press, 1992), 32.

Chapter 4

1 Ken Albala and Rosanna Nafziger, *The Lost Art of Real Cooking* (New York: Perigee, 2010), 83.

2 Ponge, "Le Pain," 33.

3 Laurel Robertson, Carol Flinders, and Bronwen Godfrey, *Laurel's Kitchen: A Handbook for Vegetarian Cookery & Nutrition* (Petaluma, CA: Nilgiri Press, 1976), 34.

4 David, *English Bread*, 92.

5 Bobrow-Strain, *White Bread*, 194.

6 Albala and Nafziger, *The Lost Art*, 85.

7 Elie Weisel, *A Passover Haggadah* (New York: Simon & Schuster, 1993), 24.

8 Joseph Tabori, *JPS Commentary on the Haggadah* (Philadelphia: Jewish Publication Society, 2008), 82.

9 Jonathan Sacks, "Sharing the Bread of Affliction," *The London Times*, March 23, 2013. It must be acknowledged, at least briefly, that this same passage goes on say that next year we shall be "in Jerusalem," a line which necessarily presents itself to contemporary hearers in the context of the vexed conflict in the Middle East; and that, therefore, may well seem to contradict the affirmation of freedom I am venturing to find in it.

10 Peter Farb and George Armelagos, *Consuming Passions: The Anthropology of Eating* (Boston: Houghton, Mifflin, 1980), 108–09; Marchant et al., *Bread*, 17.

11 Dupaigne, *History of Bread*, 156–57, 204.

12 Quoted in James Anderson Winn, *John Dryden and His World* (New Haven, CT: Yale University Press, 1987), 37, emphasis on "leavened" added.

13 John Milton, *Eikonoklastes* (London, 1645), 79.

14 Arthur Machen, *The Hill of Dreams* (London: E. Grant Richard, 1907), 278.

15 William Sewel, *The History of the Rise, Increase and Progress of the Christian People Called Quakers*, 2 vols. (New York: Baker and Crane, 1844), 1:16, emphases added.

16 Cyrus Edson, "Some Sanitary Aspects of Bread-Making," *The Cosmopolitan* 15, no. 3 (July 1893), "Advertising Supplement," 8–9, Google Books Online, accessed July 9, 2015, https://books.google.com/books?id=yWYyAQAAMAAJ&pg=RA3-PA13&lpg=RA3-PA13&dq.

17 Eugene Christian and Molly Griswold Christian, *Uncooked Foods and How to Use Them* (New York: Health Culture, 1904), 105–06.

Chapter 5

1 Alain Badiou, *Saint Paul: The Foundation of Universalism* (Stanford, CA: Stanford University Press, 2003), 13–14.

2 Ralph Waldo Emerson, Sermon 42 on Romans 14:17, in *Emerson's Prose and Poetry*, ed. Porte and Morris, 9–10.

3 Donna J. Haraway, *When Species Meet* (Minneapolis, MN: University of Minnesota Press, 2007).

Chapter 6

1 Lawrence Ferlinghetti, "The Lord's Prayer," cited from Ferlinghetti's live performance of this poem recorded in the film *The Last Waltz*, dir. Martin Scorsese (FM Productions, 1978).

2 *The Grimm Reader: The Classic Tales of the Brothers Grimm*, trans. Maria Tatar (New York: Norton, 2010), 46.

3 *Grimm Reader*, 50.

4 Camporesi, *Bread of Dreams*, 18.

5 Ibid., 56.

6 The cited line is from Karl Marx, "The Eighteenth Brumaire of Louis Bonaparte," *The Marx-Engels Reader*, 2nd edn, ed. Robert C. Tucker (New York: Norton, 1978), 595.

7 Jacob, *Six Thousand Years*, 175.

8 Toussaint-Samat, *History of Food*, 130–31; Barbara W. Tuchman, *A Distant Mirror: The Calamitous 14th Century* (New York: Random House, 1978), 183.

9 John Cleveland, *Idol of the Clownes* (London, 1654), 91.

10 William Shakespeare, *Coriolanus*, in *The Arden Shakespeare*, ed. Peter Holland (London: Bloomsbury, 2014), 150–51; on the connection of the play to the Midlands riots, sees Holland's introduction, 68–71.

11 E. P. Thompson, "The Moral Economy of the Crowd in the Eighteenth Century" (1971), in *Customs in Common* (New York: New Press, 1993), 188.

12 Quoted in Thompson, "The Moral Economy," 227.

13 Cynthia A. Bouton, *The Flour War: Gender, Class and Community in Late Ancient Régime French Society* (University Park, PA: Pennsylvania State University Press, 1993), 97.

14 Jean-Jacques Rousseau, *Les Confessions de J.J. Rousseau*, Nouvelle Édition (Paris: Charpentier, 1841), 280.

15 Henri Bergson, *Laughter*, 1899, in *Comedy*, ed. Wylie Sypher (Baltimore, MD: Johns Hopkins University Press, 1956), 155.

16 Mary Beard, *The Fires of Vesuvius: Pompeii Lost and Found* (Cambridge, MA: Harvard University Press, 2008), 171–74.

17 Jacob, *Six Thousand Years*, 129; see also Marchant et al., *Bread*, 35–37.

18 Chaucer, *General Prologue* 564, from *The Canterbury Tales*, ed. Donaldson, 24.

19 Kaplan, *Good Bread*, 14.

20 Alexander Dumas, *Dictionary of Cuisine*, ed. and trans. Louis Colman (Abingdon, OX: Routledge, 2013), 52–53.

21 Stuart Bruce Kaufman, *A Vision of Unity: The History of the Bakery and Confectionary Workers International Union* (n.p.: University of Illinois Press, 1987), 1.

22 Donald Pizer, "The Bread Line: An American Icon of Hard Times," *Studies in American Naturalism* 2, no. 2 (Winter 2007): 104.

23 Pizer, "The Bread Line," 108.

24 Theodore Dreiser, *Sister Carrie* (New York: Signet, 1961), 438, 452.

25 W. D. Howells, *Literature and Life: Studies* (New York: Harper and Sons, 1902), 154–60.

26 Pizer, "The Bread Line," 115.

27 The King James translation of this line is inexplicably awkward, so this one time I'm citing the Revised Standard Edition, *The Bible in English,* ProQuest, UC Davis Library, http:lion.chadwyck.com.

28 Dupaigne, *History of Bread*, 40.

Chapter 7

1 Mitchell Hurwitz, creator/writer, *Arrested Development* (Imagine Entertainment, Fox Television, 2003–).

2 Theresa Howard, "Atkins Nutritionals Files for Bankruptcy Protection," *USA Today*, August 1, 2005, accessed August 16, 2015, http://usatoday30.usatoday.com/money/industries/health/2005-08-01-atkins_x.htm?POE=MONISVA.

3 Lewis H. Morgan, *Ancient Society: Researches in the Lines of Human Progress from Savagery to Barbarism to Civilization* (New York: Henry Holt, 1877); Frederick Engels, *The Origins of the Family, Private Property and the State*, trans. Ernest Untermann (Chicago: Charles H. Kerr, 1902); Alvin Toffler, *The Third Wave* (New York: Macmillan, 1981).

4 Jared Diamond, "The Worst Mistake in the History of the Human Race," *Discovery Magazine,* May 1987, accessed September 5, 2015, http://discovermagazine.com/1987/may/02-the-worst-mistake-in-the-history-of-the-human-race. This essay has also been widely reprinted. See also Richard Manning, *Against the Grain: How Agriculture Has Hijacked Civilization* (New York: North Point press, 2004).

5 Marshall Sahlins, "The Original Affluent Society," in *Stone Age Economics* (New York: De Fruyter, 1972), 1–40.

6 Standage, *An Edible History*, 18.

7 Walter L. Voegtlin, *The Stone Age Diet* (New York: Vantage Press), 1975.

8 Voegtlin, *Stone Age Diet,* 4, 101, 112, 135.

9 Loren Cordain, *The Paleo Diet: Lose Weight and Get Healthy by Eating the Foods You Were Designed to Eat,* rev. edn (Boston: Houghton Mifflin Harcourt, 2011), 48–49.

10 John Durant, *The Paleo Manifesto: Ancient Wisdom for Lifelong Health* (New York: Harmony, 2014), 2, 4, 5, 7, 118.

11 Whitley, *Bread Matters*, 8–20.

12 Marlene Zuk, *Paleofantasy: What Evolution Really Tells Us About Sex, Diet and How We Live* (New York: Norton, 2013), 12, 114.

13 Karen Hardy et al., "The Importance of Dietary Carbohydrate in Human Evolution," *The Quarterly Review of Biology* 90, no. 3 (September 2015): 251–68; the cited line is from a press release about the study issued by the University of Chicago Press, accessed August 21, 2015, http://press.uchicago.edu/pressReleases/2015/August/150806_qrb_hardy_et_al_paleo_diet.html.

14 Zuk, *Paleofantasy*, 109.

15 Sindya N. Bhanoo, "Farming Had an Earlier Start, a Study Says," *New York Times*, July 27, 2015, accessed August 21, 2015, http://www.nytimes.com/2015/07/28/science/farming-had-an-earlier-start-a-study-says.html?_r=0.

16 Lauren F. Friedman, "Jimmy Kimmel Asks Gluten-Free People What Gluten Is—And Hilariously, They Have No Idea," *Business Insider*, May 9, 2014, accessed August 23, 2015, http://www.businessinsider.com/jimmy-kimmel-asks-what-is-gluten-video-2014-5#ixzz3jkl3qO7i.

17 Durant, *Paleo Manifesto*, 42–43.

18 Joseph Salama and Christina Lianos, *The Paleo Miracle: 50 Real Stories of Health Transformation* (n.p.: Paleo Miracle, 2012).

19 Alan Levinovitz, *The Gluten Lie* (Collingwood, Australia: Nero, 2015), 16, 41.

20 Whitley, *Bread Matters*, 5.

21 Kaplan, *Good Bread*, 10.

Chapter 8

1　Levinovitz, *Gluten Lie*, 26.

2　John Penkethman, *Artachthos, or A New Booke Declaring the Assise or Weight of Bread* (London, 1638), sig. A.

3　George Orwell, *Down and Out in Paris and London* (Orlando, FL: Harvest Book, 1933), 176.

4　John Ayoto, *The Oxford Book of Rhyming Slang* (Oxford: Oxford University Press, 2002), 15.

5　W. H. Auden and Christopher Isherwood, *The Dog Beneath the Skin or Where Is Frances?* (London: Faber and Faber, 1935), 123.

6　W. H. Auden, "Daily Bread," in *Juvenalia: Poems 1922–28*, ed. Katherine Bucknell (Princeton, NJ: Princeton University Press, 1994), 104–05.

7　W. H. Auden, "Horae Canonicae: Nones," in *Collected Poems*, ed. Edward Mendelsohn (New York: Vintage 1991), 634.

8　Jacob, *Six Thousand Years*, 57–58.

9　"John Barleycorn," in *The New Penguin Book of English Folk Songs*, ed. Steven Roud and Julia Bishop (New York: Penguin, 2014), 97.

10　I've been unable to determine a definitive source for this rhyme, which I first heard long ago.

11　John Wesley and Charles Wesley, *Hymns on the Lord's Supper* (London, 1825), Hymn 2, 38.

12　Pollan, *Cooked*, 52.

13　Peter Reinhart, "Forward," in H. E. Jacob, *Six Thousand Years of Bread*, vii. There seems to be a rather dark joke in the students' use of the technical term "Thermal Death Point," since this term was originally used in industrial food production to refer to the temperature required to sanitize an object or surface of potential biological contaminants such as salmonella.

Chapter 9

1 Barry Goldensohn, "Peter Schumann's Bread and Puppet Theater," *The Iowa Review* 8, no. 2 (Spring 1977): 71–73.

2 Ronald T. Simon and Marc Estrin, *Rehearsing with Gods: Photographs and Essays on the Bread & Puppet Theater* (White River Junction, VT: Chelsea Green, 2004), 186.

3 Peter Schumann, "Bread and Puppets," *The Drama Review: TDR* 14, no. 3 (1970): 35.

4 William Ralph Inge, *Christian Mysticism* (London: Methuen, 1899), 258.

5 Peter Schumann, *The Old Art of Puppetry in the New World Order: A Fiddle Lecture* (Glover, VT: Bread and Puppet Press, 1993), 6. I've written more about puppetry in *Puppets and "Popular" Culture* (Ithaca, NY: Cornell University Press, 1995).

6 Susan Bettmann, dir., *Bread: Peter Schumann and Sourdough Ryebread* (North Middlesex, VT: White Rock Productions, 2013).

7 Kaplan, *Good Bread*, 5–6.

8 Choate, *Fundamental Techniques*, 6.

9 Reinhart, *Brother Juniper's Bread Book,* 28; *The Bread-Baker's Apprentice,* 8.

10 I take this information from Thomas G. Shearman, "Our Daily Bread," *Journal of Biblical Literature* 53, no. 2 (1934): 110–17, and Herbert Thurston, "The Lord's Prayer," in *The Catholic Encyclopedia*, vol. 9 (New York: Robert Appleton Company, 1910), online version, accessed September 5, 2015, http://www.newadvent.org/cathen/09356a.htm.

11 Cited from *The Bible in English,* ProQuest, UC Davis Library, http:lion.chadwyck.com.

12 James Oppenheim's poem "Bread and Roses" was first published in 1911; today it is in the public domain and widely available in print and online, accessed September 13, 2015, for example at http://unionsong.com/u159.html.

INDEX

Page references for illustrations appear in *italics*.